READ WELL

Family Tales

Teacher's Guide

Unit 9

R**eview**

Optional 6-Day Unit

See Daily Lesson Planning, page 7

Note: See New and Important Objectives on page 2 for a complete list of skills taught and reviewed.

Critical Foundations in Primary Reading

Marilyn Sprick, Ann Watanabe, Karen Akiyama-Paik, and Shelley V. Jones

Sopris West®
EDUCATIONAL SERVICES

A Cambium Learning® Company

BOSTON, MA • LONGMONT, CO

ISBN 13-digit: 978-1-60218-532-6
ISBN 10-digit: 1-60218-532-8

7 8 9 10 11   B&B   16 15 14 13 12

166924/6-12

Table of Contents
Unit 9
Family Tales

Sequence and Sound Pronunciation Guide. iv
Introduction 1
New and Important Objectives 2
Daily Lesson Planning. 7
Materials and Materials Preparation 10
Important Tips
    Pacing: Achieving Grade Level and Above. 11

How to Teach the Lessons

Exercise 1. 14
Unit and Story Opener: Family Tales, Judith's Story 16
Vocabulary: Chapters 1, 2 18
Story Reading 1 20
    With the Teacher: Chapter 1. 20
    On Your Own: Chapter 2 25
Comprehension and Skill Activity 1: Story Comprehension. 30
Comprehension and Skill Activity 2:
    Vocabulary and Alphabetical Order. 31

Exercise 2. 32
Vocabulary: Chapters 3, 4 34
Story Reading 2 36
    With the Teacher: Chapter 3. 36
Comprehension and Skill Activity 3: Story Comprehension 40
Comprehension and Skill Activity 4: Passage Reading Fluency 41

Exercise 3. 42
Story Reading 3 44
    With the Teacher: Chapter 4. 44
    Oral Story Retell. 49
Comprehension and Skill Activity 5:
    Maze Reading and Visualization • Following Directions 50
Comprehension and Skill Activity 6:
    Main Idea and Supporting Details 51

Exercise 4 52
Story Opener: Ricardo's Stories 54
Vocabulary: Chapters 1, 2 56
Story Reading 4 58
    With the Teacher: Chapter 1 58
Comprehension and Skill Activity 7: Story Comprehension 63
Comprehension and Skill Activity 8:
    Main Idea and Supporting Details .64

Exercise 5a 66
Exercise 5b, Focus Lesson: Personal Narrative 68
Story Reading 5 70
    With the Teacher: Chapter 2 70
Comprehension and Skill Activity 9:
    Story Comprehension and Maze Reading 76
Comprehension and Skill Activity 10:
    Personal Narrative • My Story 77

Exercise 6 78
Story Reading 6 (Fluency) 80
Written Assessment 83

End of the Unit

Making Decisions: Using the Oral Reading and
    Written Assessment Results 86
Oral Reading Fluency Assessment 89
Certificate of Achievement 90

Letter Sounds and Combinations

Cumulative Review of *Read Well 1* Sounds and Combinations (Ss, Ee, ee, Mm, Aa, Dd, th, Nn, Tt, Ww, Ii, Th, Hh, Cc, Rr, ea, sh, Sh, Kk, -ck, oo, ar, wh, Wh, ĕ, -y as in fly, Ll, Oo, Bb, all, Gg, Ff, Uu, er, oo as in book, Yy, a schwa, Pp, ay, Vv, Qq, Jj, Xx, or, Zz, a_e, -y as in baby, i_e, ou, ow as in cow, ch, Ch, ai, igh, o_e, ir) and:

Unit 2	Unit 3		Unit 5	Unit 6
aw /aw/ **Paw** Voiced	**ew** /o͞o/ **Crew** Voiced	**ue** /o͞o/ **Blue** Voiced	**u_e** /o͞o/ **Flute** Bossy E Voiced	**ow** /o͞o͞o/ **Snow** Voiced (Long)	**ge** /j/ **Page** Voiced

Unit 6	Unit 7		Unit 8		Unit 10
-dge /j/ **Badge** Voiced	**ci** /sss/ **Circle** Unvoiced	**ce** /sss/ **Center** Unvoiced	**kn** /nnn/ **Knee** Voiced	**ph** /fff/ **Phone** Unvoiced	**oa** /o͞o͞o/ **Boat** Voiced (Long)

Unit 11		Unit 12		Unit 13
oi /oi/ **Point** Voiced	**ea** /ĕĕĕ/ **Bread** Voiced (Short)	**gi** /j/ **Giraffe** Voiced	**au** /au/ **Astronaut** Voiced	**oy** /oy/ **Boy** Voiced

Affixes (including morphographs—affixes taught with meaning) and Open Syllables

Cumulative Review of *Read Well 1* Affixes (-ed, -en, -es, -ing, -ly, -s, -y, -tion) and:

Unit 2	Unit 3		Unit 5	Unit 6
re- **Means again** as in <u>re</u>read	**un-** **Means not** as in <u>un</u>happy	**ex-** as in <u>ex</u>cited	**o** Open syllable /ō/ as in <u>o</u>pen and m<u>o</u>ment	**-ful** **Means full of** as in color<u>ful</u>	**bi-** **Means two** as in <u>bi</u>cycle

Unit 7	Unit 8	Unit 11	Unit 12	Unit 13	
de- as in <u>de</u>tective	**-able** as in comfort<u>able</u>	**i** Open syllable /ī/ as in s<u>i</u>lence and p<u>i</u>lot	**be-** as in <u>be</u>fore	**-ous** as in enorm<u>ous</u>	**dis-** as in <u>dis</u>cover

Unit 14		Unit 15		Unit 16	
-al as in anim<u>al</u>	**-ible** as in flex<u>ible</u>	**-or** **Means one who** as in act<u>or</u>	**-ment** as in apart<u>ment</u>	**-ic** as in scientif<u>ic</u>	**pre-** **Means before** as in <u>pre</u>view

Unit 17		Unit 18		Unit 19	
-ity as in activ<u>ity</u>	**-sion** as in permis<u>sion</u>	**-ness** as in fair<u>ness</u>	**-less** **Means without** as in help<u>less</u>	**in-** as in <u>in</u>sert	**im-** **Means not** as in <u>im</u>possible

Introduction
Family Tales

Story Notes

Unit 9 is a collection of personal narratives that illustrate the importance of family connections. A real family shares stories that honor two cultures, two countries, and multiple generations. In the process, students revisit the themes of immigration and storytelling from earlier units.

Judith's Story: "What is that?" Judith asks her mother, looking out the window and pointing to the tall buildings. Enjoy Judith's candid observations when she and her family immigrate to the United States from a rural Mexican town.

Ricardo's Stories: Ricardo shares three family stories that he tells his own children. Students will find humor in "Grandmother's Cow" and enjoy reading about Ricardo's first visit to Mexico.

Recommended Read Alouds

Suggested Read Alouds enhance small group instruction—providing opportunities to further build background knowledge and vocabulary. Read aloud outside the reading block.

The Wednesday Surprise by Eve Bunting
Fiction • Narrative
Everyone thinks Grandma is teaching her granddaughter Anna to read, but it's really the other way around.

Aunt Flossie's Hats (and Crab Cakes Later)
by Elizabeth Fitzgerald Howard
Fiction • Narrative
Great-great-aunt Flossie is a storyteller. She has a story to go with each hat she owns!

Too Many Tamales by Gary Soto
Fiction • Narrative
Maria feels grown-up when she is allowed to knead the *masa* for holiday tamales, but trouble starts when she tries on her mother's diamond ring.

Read Well Connections
The Read Alouds feature family stories and traditions from three different cultures. These stories reinforce the wonderful traditions found in different cultures.

NOTE FROM THE AUTHORS

Every immigrant has his or her own story. Each story is unique.

Judith and Ricardo each have doctoral degrees in school psychology. As dedicated educators, they have graciously shared their stories and experiences as an immigrant and son of an immigrant. Our deepest appreciation to Judith, Ricardo, and their children—Isabel and Daniel—for sharing their stories.

New and Important Objectives
A Research-Based Reading Program

Phonemic Awareness
Phonics
Fluency
Vocabulary
Comprehension

Phonological and Phonemic Awareness
Blending; Rhyming; Onset and Rime; Counting Syllables

Phonics
Cumulative Letter Sounds and Combinations
Review • Ss, Ee, ee, Mm, Aa, Dd, th, Nn, Tt, Ww, Ii, Th, Hh, Cc, Rr, ea, sh, Sh, Kk, -ck, oo, ar, wh, Wh, ĕ, -y (as in fly), Ll, Oo, Bb, all, Gg, Ff, Uu, er, oo (as in book), Yy, a (schwa), Pp, ay, Vv, Qq, Jj, Xx, or, Zz, a_e, -y (as in baby), i_e, ou, ow (as in cow), ch, Ch, ai, igh, o_e, ir, aw, ew, ue, u_e, ow (as in snow), ge, -dge, ci, ce, kn, ph

Cumulative Affixes, Morphographs, and Open Syllables
Review • -ed, -en, -er, -es, -est, -ing, -ly, -s, -y, -tion, re-, un-, ex-, o (as in open), -ful, bi-, de-, -able

★New Proper Nouns
Daniel, Daniel's, Isabel, Judith, Judith's, Papa, Papa's, Ricardo, Thanksgiving

★New Pattern Words
blond, church, crow, greeted, mane, pan, ranch, shoo, speak, steer, tile

*Known Pattern Words With Affixes • baking, cows, frying, growing, kisses, knows, lawns, names, rerun, sleepily, smiles, stores, tallest, untrue, waking, waved, yards

---

* **Known Pattern Words With Affixes, Known Tricky Words With Affixes,** and **Known Multisyllabic Words With Affixes** have base words students have previously read. The words are new in this unit because they have not been previously read with the affix.

★ = New in this unit

Phonics (*continued*)

☆ **New Compound and Hyphenated Words**

doorway, somebody, someday, whenever

☆ **Other New Multisyllabic Words**

candy, drowsy, elevator, elevators, ladder, mommy, okay, ruckus, stubby

　 ***Known Multisyllabic Words With Affixes** • chuckling, cities, funnier, giggles, husband's, immigrated, rumbling, teachers

☆ **New Spanish Words**

abuela, abuelo, buenos días, delicioso, hola, mami, papa, papi, qué

☆ **New Tricky Words**

already, climb, education, glisten, none, permission, toward, wandered

　 ***Known Tricky Words With Affixes** • laughs, listens, quietly, touched

Fluency

Accuracy, Expression, Phrasing, Rate

Vocabulary

New • drowsy, glisten, immigrate, permission

Review • bittersweet, commotion, generation, immigrant, tradition, village

Reviewed in Context • ancient, belongings, bittersweet, commotion, cram, distressed, imagine, immigrant, relative, scrumptious, tradition, village, wonderful

Comprehension

Unit Genres

Nonfiction • Personal Narrative

Comprehension Processes

Build Knowledge: Factual, Procedural, Conceptual

Day	1	2	3	4	5	6
Remember						
Defining						
Identifying (recalling)	S,C	S,C	S,C	S,C	E,S,C	C
Using	C	S	S			
Understand						
Defining (in your own words)	S,C			C	S	C
Describing	S					
Explaining (rephrasing)	S	S	S	S		
Illustrating	C		C	C	C	
Sequencing					C	C
Summarizing	S	S	S			
Using	S,C	S		S,C	S,C	C
Visualizing	C		C	C	C	
Apply						
Demonstrating						
Explaining (unstated)	S	S	S	S	S	S,C
Illustrating			C			
Inferring	S	S	S	S	S,C	S,C
Making Connections (relating)	S,C	S,C				
Predicting		S	S	S	S	
Using	S,C			S	S	
Analyze						
Classifying						
Comparing/Contrasting		S	S			
Distinguishing Cause/Effect						
Drawing Conclusions				S		
Inferring	S					
Evaluate						
Making Judgments						
Responding (personal)			S	S	S	
Create						
Generating Ideas		S,C			E,C	

E = Exercise, S = Storybook, C = Comprehension & Skill

4

Comprehension (continued)

Skills and Strategies

Day	1	2	3	4	5	6
Priming Background Knowledge						
Setting a Purpose for Reading	S					
Answering Questions	S	S	S	S	S	S
Asking Questions						
Visualizing						
Comprehension Monitoring/Fix Ups						
Does it Make Sense?	C	C	C	C	C	
Looking Back						
Restating						
Summarizing						
Main Idea						
Retelling			S			
Supporting Details			C			
Understanding Text Structure						
Title, Author, Illustrator	S		S	S	S	
Fact or Fiction						
Genre (Classifying)						
Narrative						
Setting			S	S,C	S	S
Main Character/Traits (Characterization)*	S,C		S			C*
Goal	S					
Problem/Solution						
Action/Events/Sequence					C	C
Outcome/Conclusion			S			C
Lesson/Author's Message						
Expository						
Subject/Topic			C	C		
Heading						
Supporting Details (Facts/Information)				C		
Main Idea			C	C		C
Using Graphic Organizers						
Chart						
Diagram (labeling)						
Hierarchy (topic/detail)			C	C		
K-W-L						
Map (locating, labeling)						
Matrix (compare/contrast)		C				
Sequence (linear, cycle, cause and effect)						
Story Map						
Web						

E = Exercise, S = Storybook, C = Comprehension & Skill

* Narrator

5

Comprehension (continued)

Study Skills

Day	1	2	3	4	5	6
Alphabetical Order	C					
Following Directions			C			
Locating Information						
Note Taking						
Previewing	S					
Reviewing		S	S		S	
Test Taking			C		C	C
Using Glossary						
Using Table of Contents	S			S		
Viewing						
Verifying						

Writing in Response to Reading

Day	1	2	3	4	5	6
Sentence Completion	C	C	C	C	C	C
Making Lists		C				
Sentence Writing	C		C			C
Story Retell/Summary			S			
Fact Summary						
Paragraph Writing					C	
Report Writing						
Open-Ended Response	C					
Creative Writing					C	

Writing Traits

(Addressed within the context of Writing in Response to Reading)

Day	1	2	3	4	5	6
Ideas and Content						
Elaborating/Generating					S,C	
Organization						
Introduction						
Topic Sentence						
Supporting Details			C	C		
Sequencing			S		C	
Word Choice						
Sophisticated Words (Tier 2 and 3)						
Conventions						
Capital	C		C	C	C	C
Ending Punctuation	C			C	C	C
Other (commas, quotation marks)			C			
Presentation						
Handwriting	C	C	C	C	C	
Neatness	C				C	

E = Exercise, S = Storybook, C = Comprehension & Skill

Daily Lesson Planning

OPTIONAL REVIEW AND ENRICHMENT UNIT

- **High-Performing Groups:** Do Unit 9 if your group is on pace to complete Unit 19 or higher by the end of the students' second grade year. The content of Unit 9 provides enrichment.
- **Average-Performing Groups:** Skip this unit if your students are meeting fluency requirements and may not complete Unit 19 by the end of the year.
- **Lower-Performing Groups:** Do this unit if some students are barely meeting fluency requirements. Though the content of Unit 9 provides enrichment, the review of skills is important for students who need additional time to firm up known skills.

LESSON PLAN FORMAT

Teacher-Directed 45 Minutes		Independent Teacher-Directed, as needed
Lesson Part 1 (Phonological Awareness, Phonics, Fluency, Comprehension) 15–20 Minutes	**Lesson Part 2** (Vocabulary, Fluency, Comprehension) 20–25 Minutes	**Lesson Part 3** (Vocabulary, Fluency, Comprehension) 15–20 Minutes
• Exercises	• Unit and/or Story Opener • Vocabulary • Interactive Story Reading • Short Passage Practice Timed Readings	• Story Reading With Partner or Whisper Reading • Comprehension and Skill Activities

HOMEWORK

Read Well Homework (blackline masters of new *Read Well 2* passages) provides an opportunity for children to celebrate accomplishments with parents. Homework should be sent home on routine days.

ORAL READING FLUENCY ASSESSMENT

Upon completion of this unit, assess each student and proceed to Unit 10, as appropriate.

WRITTEN ASSESSMENT

During the time students would normally complete Comprehension and Skill Activities, students will be administered a Written Assessment that can be found on page 63 in the student's *Activity Book 2*.

DIFFERENTIATED LESSON PLANS

The differentiated lesson plans illustrate how to use materials for students with various learning needs. As you set up your unit plan, always include *Read Well 2* Exercises and Story Reading on a daily basis. Unit 9 includes 6- and 8-Day Plans.

Plans	For groups that:
6-DAY	Complete Oral Reading Fluency Assessments with Passes and Strong Passes
8-DAY	Complete Oral Reading Fluency Assessments with Passes and require teacher-guided assistance with Story Reading and Comprehension and Skill Work

6-DAY PLAN

Day 1	Day 2	Day 3
Teacher-Directed • Exercise 1 • Unit and Story Opener: Family Tales, Judith's Story • Vocabulary, Ch. 1, 2 • Judith's Story, Ch. 1 • Guide practice, as needed, on Comp & Skill 1, 2 **Independent Work** • On Your Own: Partner or Whisper Read, Judith's Story, Ch. 2 • Comp & Skill 1, 2 **Homework** • Homework Passage 1	**Teacher-Directed** • Exercise 2 • Vocabulary, Ch. 3 • Judith's Story, Ch. 3 • Guide practice, as needed, on Comp & Skill 3, 4 **Independent Work** • Repeated Reading: Partner or Whisper Read, Judith's Story, Ch. 3 • Comp & Skill 3, 4 **Homework** • Homework Passage 2	**Teacher-Directed** • Exercise 3 • Judith's Story, Ch. 4 • Story Retell • Guide practice, as needed, on Comp & Skill 5, 6 **Independent Work** • Repeated Reading: Partner or Whisper Read, Judith's Story, Ch. 4 • Comp & Skill 5, 6 **Homework** • Homework Passage 3
Day 4	**Day 5**	**Day 6**
Teacher-Directed • Exercise 4 • Story Opener: Ricardo's Stories • Vocabulary, Ch. 1, 2 • Ricardo's Stories, Ch. 1 • Guide practice, as needed, on Comp & Skill 7, 8 **Independent Work** • Repeated Reading: Partner or Whisper Read, Ricardo's Stories, Ch. 1 • Comp & Skill 7, 8 **Homework** • Homework Passage 4	**Teacher-Directed** • Exercise 5a • Exercise 5b: Focus Lesson • Ricardo's Stories, Ch. 2 • Guide practice, as needed, on Comp & Skill 9, 10 **Independent Work** • Repeated Reading: Partner or Whisper Read, Ricardo's Stories, Ch. 2 • Comp & Skill 9, 10 **Homework** • Homework Passage 5	**Teacher-Directed** • Exercise 6 • Fluency, Fudge **Independent Work** • Repeated Reading: Partner or Whisper Read, Fudge • Written Assessment • Oral Reading Fluency Assessment* **Homework** • Homework Passage 6

* The Oral Reading Fluency Assessments are individually administered by the teacher while students are working on their Written Assessments.

Day 1	Day 2	Day 3	Day 4
Teacher-Directed	**Teacher-Directed**	**Teacher-Directed**	**Teacher-Directed**
• Exercise 1	• Review Exercise 1	• Exercise 2	• Exercise 3
• Unit and Story Opener: Family Tales, Judith's Story	• Review Vocabulary, Ch. 1, 2	• Vocabulary, Ch. 3	• Judith's Story, Ch. 4
• Vocabulary, Ch. 1, 2	• Judith's Story, Ch. 2	• Judith's Story, Ch. 3	• Story Retell
• Judith's Story, Ch. 1	• Guide practice, as needed, on Comp & Skill 2	• Guide practice, as needed, on Comp & Skill 3, 4	• Guide practice, as needed, on Comp & Skill 5, 6
• Guide practice, as needed, on Comp & Skill 1	**Independent Work**	**Independent Work**	**Independent Work**
Independent Work	• Repeated Reading: Partner or Whisper Read, Judith's Story, Ch. 2	• Repeated Reading: Partner or Whisper Read, Judith's Story, Ch. 3	• Repeated Reading: Partner or Whisper Read, Judith's Story, Ch. 4
• Repeated Reading: Partner or Whisper Read, Judith's Story, Ch. 1	• Comp & Skill 2	• Comp & Skill 3, 4	• Comp & Skill 5, 6
• Comp & Skill 1	**Homework**	**Homework**	**Homework**
Homework	• Homework Passage 2	• Homework Passage 3	• Homework Passage 4
• Homework Passage 1			

Day 5	Day 6	Day 7	Day 8
Teacher-Directed	**Teacher-Directed**	**Teacher-Directed**	**Teacher-Directed**
• Exercise 4	• Exercise 5a	• Review Exercise 5a	• Exercise 6
• Story Opener: Ricardo's Stories	• Ricardo's Stories, Ch. 2	• Exercise 5b: Focus Lesson	• Fluency, Fudge
• Vocabulary, Ch. 1, 2	• Guide practice, as needed, on Comp & Skill 9	• Reread Ricardo's Stories, Ch. 2	**Independent Work**
• Ricardo's Stories, Ch. 1	**Independent Work**	• Guide practice, as needed, on Comp & Skill 10	• Repeated Reading: Fluency, Fudge
• Guide practice, as needed, on Comp & Skill 7, 8	• Repeated Reading: Partner or Whisper Read, Ricardo's Stories, Ch. 2	**Independent Work**	• Written Assessment
Independent Work	• Comp & Skill 9	• Repeated Reading: Partner or Whisper Read, Ricardo's Stories, Ch. 2	• Oral Reading Fluency Assessment*
• Repeated Reading: Partner or Whisper Read, Ricardo's Stories, Ch. 1	**Homework**	• Comp & Skill 10	**Homework**
• Comp & Skill 7, 8	• Comp & Skill 4 (Passage Reading Fluency)	**Homework**	• Teacher's Choice
Homework		• Homework Passage 6	
• Homework Passage 5			

Materials and Materials Preparation

Core Lessons

Teacher Materials

READ WELL 2 MATERIALS

- Unit 9 Teacher's Guide
- Sound Cards
- Unit 9 Oral Reading Fluency Assessment found on page 89
- Group Assessment Record found in the *Assessment Manual*

SCHOOL SUPPLIES

Stopwatch or watch with a second hand

Student Materials

READ WELL 2 MATERIALS (for each student)

- *From Generation to Generation* storybook
- *Exercise Book 2*
- *Activity Book 2* or copies of Unit 9 Comprehension and Skill Work
- Unit 9 Written Assessment found in *Activity Book 2*, page 63, and on the blackline master CD
- Unit 9 Certificate of Achievement (BLM, page 90)
- Unit 9 Homework (blackline masters)
  See *Getting Started* for suggested homework routines.

SCHOOL SUPPLIES

Pencils, colors (optional—markers, crayons, or colored pencils)

> Make one copy per student of each blackline master, as appropriate for the group.
>
> *Note:* For new or difficult Comprehension and Skill Activities, make overhead transparencies from the blackline masters. Use the transparencies to demonstrate and guide practice.

> **FOCUS LESSON**
>
> For Exercise 5b (Focus Lesson), make overhead transparencies from the blackline masters, write on transparencies placed over the pages, or use paper copies to demonstrate how to complete the lesson.
>
> demonstrate how to complete the lessons.

> **CAUTION**
> Use these lessons only if needed. Students who need Extra Practice may benefit from one, two, or three lessons.

Important Tips

Pacing: Achieving Grade Level and Above

*Mastery learning takes precedence
over simply getting through the program.*

REACHING GRADE LEVEL AND ABOVE

Students are likely to be at or above grade level as measured by a standardized test if, by the end of the school year, they complete Unit 19, *Flat Stanley,* and have met passing requirements for each *Read Well* Oral Reading Fluency Assessment. We encourage you to aim for Unit 20 or higher by the end of the year.

AUTHORS' NOTE ON GRADE LEVEL

Grade level and grade level expectations are measured in a variety of ways. Rate of progress through the program should not be your only measure of grade level.

Using the chart that follows and a school calendar, you can calculate approximately where your students will be by the end of the school year. If there are not enough days in the school year to complete Unit 19 with mastery, the following variables can be manipulated:

Skip Unit 9

Unit 9 is a review unit. If, and only if, your students are *easily* passing the Oral Reading Fluency Assessments, this unit could be skipped or read by students independently, outside of the instructional reading period.

INCREASE INSTRUCTIONAL TIME

Work with your colleagues to:

• increase time in the instructional reading block for each group.

• reduce interruptions—teach five days per week.

• maintain program fidelity.

Adhere to lessons!

For low-performing groups, add a second instructional period in the afternoon.

In this instance, the double dose would be for the purpose of moving the group forward faster, with two teachers coordinating instruction. See Section 4.4 in *Getting Started* for more information on double dosing.

PACING CHART			
Theme	**Unit No.**	**Unit**	**Days in Core Plan**
Our World, Our Home	1	Maya and Ben	6
	2	Mapping Our World	6
	3	African Adventures	6
Communities	4	Arthur's Pet Business*	2
	5	Life as an Ant	6
	6	Sir Henry	6
	7	Stories from Hilo	6
From Generation to Generation	8	Traditional Tales	7
	9	Family Tales*	6
All About Dinosaurs	10	Dino Discoveries	6
	11	Dog Detective	6
	12	Dinosaurs Before Dark	10
Spiders and Bats	13	Spiders	8
	14	Bats	6
Young America	15	Snapshots of American West	6
	16	Wild, Wild West	6
Interdependence	17	RW Science Digest Vol. 1: Food Chains	6
	18	The Reef	6
Imagination	19	Flat Stanley	7
	20	MSB: Inside the Human Body	6

> **WHERE YOU ARE NOW**
>
> If you are following the core plans and teach Unit 9, your group will require about 73 more days of instruction to complete Unit 19 and reach at least a beginning third grade level.

> **GRADE LEVEL**
>
> Grade level is not a standard concept and is determined in a variety of ways. Our field test results indicated that students scored at least a 3.0 in grade equivalence when completing Unit 19.
>
> *Many students scored higher.*

Inspiring People	21	A Great Man	6
	22	Thomas Edison: A Brilliant Inventor	8
Earth We Share	23	RW Science Digest Vol. 2: Where in the World?	8
	24	Judy Moody Saves the World!	12
Mystery	25	The Absent Author	9

If your students placed in *RW2* Unit 5 or higher at the beginning of the school year, you may find that you have additional time at the end of the school year for another trade book study of your choice.

* Review Unit

How to Teach the Lessons

Teach from this section. Each instructional component is outlined in an easy-to-teach format.

Exercise 1

- Unit and Story Opener:
  Family Tales, Judith's Story
- Vocabulary
- Story Reading 1
  With the Teacher: Chapter 1
  On Your Own: Chapter 2
- Comprehension and Skill Activities 1, 2

Exercise 2

- Vocabulary
- Story Reading 2
  With the Teacher: Chapter 3
- Comprehension and Skill Activities 3, 4

Exercise 3

- Story Reading 3
  With the Teacher: Chapter 4
- Story Retell
- Comprehension and Skill Activities 5, 6

Exercise 4

- Story Opener: Ricardo's Stories
- Vocabulary
- Story Reading 4
  With the Teacher: Chapter 1
- Comprehension and Skill Activities 7, 8

Exercise 5a

- Exercise 5b: Focus Lesson
- Story Reading 5
  With the Teacher: Chapter 2
- Comprehension and Skill Activities 9, 10

Exercise 6

- Story Reading 6
  With the Teacher: Fudge (Fluency)
- Written Assessment

Note: Lessons include daily homework.

❶ SOUND REVIEW

Use selected Sound Cards from Units 1–8.

PACING

Exercise 1 should take about 15 minutes.

❷ ACCURACY AND FLUENCY BUILDING

• For each task, have students say any underlined part, then read the word.

• Set a pace. Then have students read the whole words in each task and column.

• Provide repeated practice, building accuracy first, then fluency.

B2. Names and Places

For words that students may be able to sound out, have students figure out the word, then put their thumbs up when they know the word.

E1. Tricky Words

• For each Tricky Word, have students use the sounds and word parts they know to silently sound out the word. Use the word in a sentence to help with pronunciation.

touched	The teacher said, "Simon says touch your ear." So I . . . *touched* . . . my ear.
enough	Dad asked, "Do you want more?" I said, "No thanks. I've had . . . *enough*."
believe	That funny story was hard to . . . *believe*.
goes	There he . . . *goes*.
listens	Sam learns because he always . . . *listens*.
lived	The ancient turtle had . . . *lived* . . . for 200 years.
able	Can you do it? Are you . . . *able*?

• Have students go back and read the whole words in the column.

❸ MULTISYLLABIC WORDS

For each word, have students read the syllables, then the whole word. Use the word in a sentence, as appropriate.

elevators	Most tall buildings have . . . *elevators*.
generation	People my age belong to my . . . *generation*.
immigrate	When you move to another country, you . . . *immigrate* . . . to that country.
immigrating	Patrice's family was moving to the United States. They were . . . *immigrating* . . . to the United States.
remember	My teacher asked me a question, but I couldn't . . . *remember* . . . the answer.
belongings	When she was ready to move, she packed her . . . *belongings*.

❹ MORPHOGRAPHS AND AFFIXES

★❺ SPANISH WORDS

• Tell students they will be reading Spanish words. Have students point to the word as it is pronounced. Model how to say the word. If you have Spanish-speaking students in the group, have them model. Say something like:
Look at the first word. It means grandmother in Spanish. Now look at the way the word is pronounced. Listen to me say it. ah-bway-lah. Now you say the word. (Abuela)

• Have students read the translation. (Abuela means Grandmother.)

★ = New in this unit

⑥ **GENERALIZATION: READING NEW WORDS IN PARAGRAPHS**
- Have students read the paragraph silently, then out loud. Tell students to use the sounds and word parts they know to read any difficult words.
- Repeat practice, as needed.

Judith's Story

Unit 9 Exercise 1
Use before Chapters 1 and 2

1. SOUND REVIEW Use selected Sound Cards from Units 1–8.

2. ACCURACY AND FLUENCY BUILDING For each column, have students say any underlined part, then read each word. Next, have students read the whole column.

A1 Mixed Practice	**B1** Bossy E	**C1** Word Endings	**D1** Buildups	**E1** Tricky Words
<u>k</u>nows	<u>na</u>mes	<u>tallest</u>	sleep	touched
just	sm<u>i</u>les	cra<u>mm</u>ed	sleepy	enough
pr<u>ou</u>d	l<u>i</u>ke	<u>buttons</u>	sleepily	believe
wind<u>ow</u>	**B2** Names and Places	wake	**D2** Story Words	goes
villa<u>ge</u>	Isabel	waking	already	listens
w<u>ai</u>ted	Judith	city	qui<u>e</u>t	lived
<u>a</u>sleep	Daniel	cities	<u>f</u>inally	able
	Ricardo			
	Mexico			

3. MULTISYLLABIC WORDS Have students read each word part, then read each whole word.

Ⓐ	el•e•va•tors	elevators	gen•er•a•tion	generation
Ⓑ	im•mi•grate	immigrate	im•mi•grat•ing	immigrating
Ⓒ	re•mem•ber	remember	be•long•ings	belongings

4. MORPHOGRAPHS AND AFFIXES Have students read each underlined word part, then the word.

<u>ex</u>plain	real<u>ly</u>	question<u>s</u>	lik<u>able</u>	<u>de</u>cide

5. SPANISH WORDS Have students read the word using the pronunciation guide. Then have students read the sentence that tells what the word means.

Ⓐ	Abuela	Ah-bway-lah	<u>Abuela</u> means Grandmother.
Ⓑ	Abuelo	Ah-bway-loh	<u>Abuelo</u> means Grandfather.
Ⓒ	Mami	Mah-mee	<u>Mami</u> means Mommy.

6. GENERALIZATION Have students read the paragraph silently, then out loud. (New words: Isabel, church, permission, okay)

Isabel was excited. Mrs. Martinez and her husband had a new baby. Isabel sat quietly until church was over, then asked her mom for permission to go see the baby. The baby was just waking up. Isabel asked, "Would it be okay for me to hold the baby?"

TEAM EXPECTATIONS

Acknowledge Team Efforts (Reminder)

Pair your compliments with team expectations. Say something like:

[Raj], I like the way you followed directions.

[Akiko], you are sitting up so I can hear your great reading.

GENERALIZATION (Reminder)

The generalization task provides an opportunity for you to informally assess students' ability to read new words that have not been pretaught.

COMPREHENSION PROCESSES

Remember, Understand, Apply

PROCEDURES

1. **Introducing the Unit and Story**

   Using the Table of Contents; Identifying—Titles, Narrator, Main Character; Inferring

   Tell students the title of their new unit and story.
   Say something like:

   Everyone, turn to page 4. What's on this page? (the Table of Contents)
   The title of our new unit is "Family Tales." Touch the unit title. What's the title of this unit? (Family Tales)

   Find the first story in the unit. What is it called?
   (Judith's Story)
   Who do you think is going to be the narrator in this story? (Judith)
   That's right. The story is told by Judith.

TABLE OF CONTENTS
UNIT 9 • Family Tales

Judith's Story 49
PERSONAL NARRATIVE

With the Teacher
Vocabulary: Chapters 1, 2 50
Chapter 1, Immigrating to the United States 52

On Your Own
Chapter 2, The Tall Buildings 56

With the Teacher
Vocabulary: Chapters 3, 4 60
Chapter 3, Going to School in America 61

With the Teacher
Chapter 4, Lovely Green Lawns 64
STORY RETELL 68

UNIT 9
Family Tales

Judith's Story **49**

a personal narrative
by Judith Plasencia-Peinado, Ph.D.
illustrated by Johanna Van Der Sterre

Ricardo's Stories **69**

a personal narrative
by Ricardo Peinado, Ph.D.
illustrated by Johanna Van Der Sterre

Judith and Ricardo both grew up in California. They worked hard in school, went to college, and earned their doctorates in school psychology.

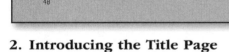

48

Judith's Story

a personal narrative
by Judith Plasencia-Peinado, Ph.D.
illustrated by Johanna Van Der Sterre

From *generation* to generation, families grow, move, and experience new things. Every family has its own stories, and every story is special.

In this unit, you will meet Judith and Ricardo. They are real people with their own special stories. We are happy that they have shared their stories with us. After you finish reading this unit, we hope you will share your own stories with your classmates.

49

2. Introducing the Title Page

Inferring; Explaining; Identifying— Illustrator

- Have students look at the picture on page 48. Explain to students that this is an illustration of the authors, Judith and Ricardo, and their family.
- Read the gray text on page 48.
- Have students look at the title page.
  Everyone, turn to page 49, the title page.
  This is how the artist has drawn Judith. Who is the artist?
  (Johanna Van Der Sterre)

- Read the gray text at the bottom of the page.
- After reading the gray text, say something like:
  I think you are going to enjoy this story. At the end of this unit, you get to write your own story. It will be fun to read your story.

COMPREHENSION PROCESSES

Understand

PROCEDURES

Introducing Vocabulary

> ★ **immigrate** ★ **permission, generation**

- For each vocabulary word, have students read the word by parts, then read the whole word.
- Read the student-friendly explanations to students as they follow with their fingers. Then have students use the vocabulary word by following the gray text.
- Review and discuss the photos.

USING VOCABULARY

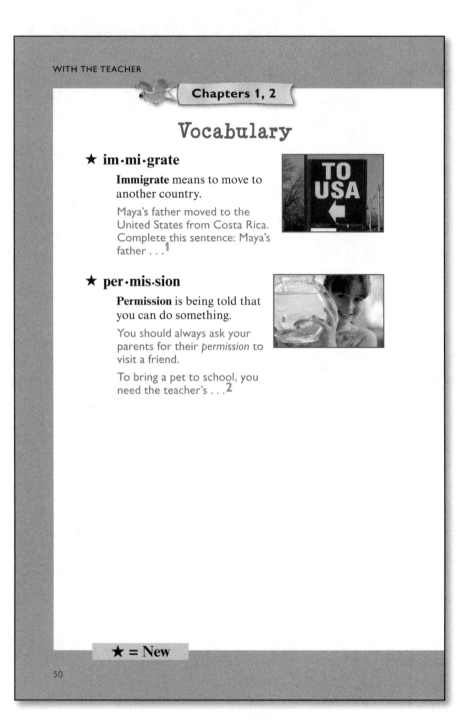

WITH THE TEACHER

Chapters 1, 2

Vocabulary

★ **im·mi·grate**

Immigrate means to move to another country.

Maya's father moved to the United States from Costa Rica. Complete this sentence: Maya's father . . .[1]

★ **per·mis·sion**

Permission is being told that you can do something.

You should always ask your parents for their *permission* to visit a friend.

To bring a pet to school, you need the teacher's . . .[2]

★ = New

50

❶ Understand: Using Vocabulary—immigrate (immigrated to the United States)
❷ Understand: Using Vocabulary—permission (permission)

★ = New in this unit

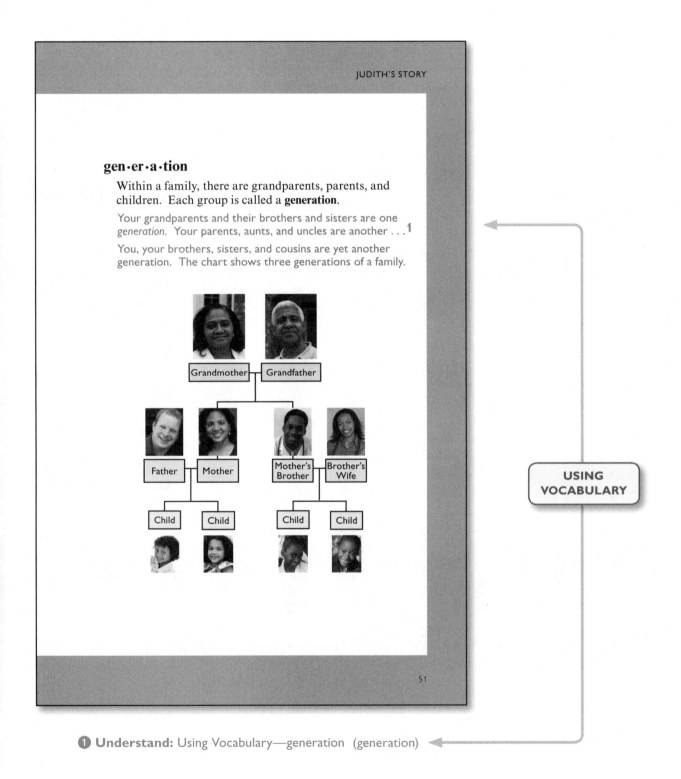

JUDITH'S STORY

gen·er·a·tion

Within a family, there are grandparents, parents, and children. Each group is called a **generation**.

Your grandparents and their brothers and sisters are one *generation*. Your parents, aunts, and uncles are another . . .¹

You, your brothers, sisters, and cousins are yet another generation. The chart shows three generations of a family.

Grandmother — Grandfather

Father — Mother   Mother's Brother — Brother's Wife

Child   Child   Child   Child

51

❶ **Understand:** Using Vocabulary—generation (generation)

USING VOCABULARY

CHAPTER 1 INSTRUCTIONS

Students read Chapter 1 with the teacher and Chapter 2 on their own. *Note*: If you're working on an 8-Day Plan, you will read Chapter 2 with students.

COMPREHENSION PROCESSES

Remember, Understand, Apply

COMPREHENSION BUILDING

• Encourage students to answer questions with complete sentences.
• If students have difficulty comprehending, think aloud with them or reread the portion of the story that answers the question. Repeat the question.

PROCEDURES

1. **Introducing Chapter 1**

   Identifying—Who; Inferring; Defining Vocabulary—immigrate
   Have students read the title, then say something like:
   We think that Judith is going to narrate this story.
   Who do you think immigrated to the United States? (Judith)
   What does that mean? (She came from another country.)
   Where do you think Judith is from?

2. **First Reading**
   • Ask questions and discuss the story as indicated by the gray text.
   • Mix group and individual turns, independent of your voice.
     Have students work toward a group accuracy goal of 0–3 errors.
     Quietly keep track of errors made by all students in the group.
   • After reading the story, practice any difficult words.
     Reread the story if students have not reached the accuracy goal.

3. **Second Reading, Short Passage Practice: Developing Prosody**
   • Demonstrate expressive, fluent reading of the first paragraph.
     Read at a rate slightly faster than the students' rate. Say something like:
     In the introduction, Judith is talking. I think Judith would have a soft gentle voice. That's the way I imagine Judith. Listen to me read as if I were Judith.

     "Hello. My name is Judith. My husband, Ricardo, and I have two children. Their names are Isabel and Daniel. They like me to tell them about immigrating to the United States."

   • Guide practice with your voice.
   • Provide individual turns while others track with their fingers and whisper read.
   • Repeat with one paragraph at a time. Repeat steps with each remaining paragraph.

CORRECTING DECODING ERRORS

During story reading, gently correct any error, then have students reread the sentence.

REPEATED READINGS

Prosody

On the second reading, students practice developing prosody— phrasing and expression. Research has shown that prosody is related to both fluency and comprehension.

WITH THE TEACHER

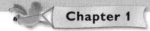 Chapter 1

Immigrating to the United States

Hello. My name is Judith. My husband, Ricardo, and I have two children. Their names are Isabel and Daniel. They like me to tell them about immigrating to the United States. Isabel says, "Mami, tell me about when you were seven. Tell me how you came to the United States from Mexico." Isabel often says this when it is time to go to bed!

Who is telling the story?[1]

52

COMPREHENDING AS YOU GO

❶ **Remember:** Identifying—Narrator, Main Character (Judith is telling the story.)
We were right. Judith is the narrator.

JUDITH'S STORY

I say to Isabel, "You already know this story, and it is time to go to bed."

Isabel says, "Yes, but tell me again."

I look at the clock and say, "Okay. We have just enough time."

Isabel smiles, and I begin. "Do you remember how old I was?"

Isabel says, "Yes, Mami. You were seven."

Why do you think Isabel asked to hear her mother's story again?[1]

53

COMPREHENDING
AS YOU GO

❶ Apply: Inferring, Making Connections (Isabel likes the story. Isabel doesn't want to go to bed . . .)

WITH THE TEACHER

"That's right. I was seven when we came from Mexico. We waited a long time to come to this country. It took many years for your grandmother and grandfather to get permission to come to the United States."

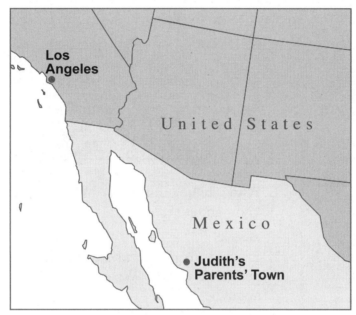

Judith and her family immigrated to the
United States nearly 40 years ago.

Isabel asks, "Why did Abuela (Ah-bway-lah) and Abuelo (Ah-bway-loh) have to get permission to come here?"

How old was Judith when she moved to the United States?[1] How long ago was that?[2]

54

COMPREHENDING
AS YOU GO

❶ **Remember:** Identifying—How Old (Judith was seven when she came to the United States.)

❷ **Understand:** Explaining (It was many years ago. Judith is now an adult with kids of her own.)

JUDITH'S STORY

Isabel asks many questions. Soon she will be able to tell my story. Daniel is still very little. He doesn't ask questions, but he listens very carefully.

I explain, "Abuelo and Abuela were born in Mexico. They wanted to work in the United States, so they needed to get permission from this country to come and work."

Think and Talk

NARRATOR

1. Who is telling this story? What do you know about her?

INFERENCE

2. It sounds like Isabel and Daniel have a bedtime tradition. What do you think it might be?

INFERENCE

3. Why do you think Judith is happy to tell her story over and over again?

EXPLANATION

4. Why did Judith's family want to immigrate, or move, to the United States?

55

❶ **Remember:** Identifying—Narrator; **Understand:** Describing—Character Traits (Characterization) (Judith is telling the story. She is from Mexico. She is nice and patient with her children.)

❷ **Apply:** Inferring; Explaining; Using Vocabulary—tradition (Their bedtime tradition is to listen to a story.)

❸ **Apply:** Inferring—Goal; Explaining (She likes telling the story. The story is important to her. She likes making her children happy. She wants her children to be able to retell her story.)

❹ **Understand:** Explaining (They wanted to work in the United States.)

CHAPTER 2 INSTRUCTIONS

Students read without the teacher, independently or with partners.
Note: If you're working on an 8-Day Plan, you will read Chapter 2
with students.

COMPREHENSION PROCESSES

Remember, Apply, Analyze

PROCEDURES FOR READING ON YOUR OWN

1. Getting Ready

Have students turn to "Judith's Story," Chapter 2 on page 56.

2. Setting a Purpose

Identifying—Title, Where; Previewing; Explaining; Summarizing
Before students begin reading, say something like:
What's the title of Chapter 2? (The Tall Buildings)
Read to find out the answers to these questions:
  • Where did Judith live before she moved to the United States?
  • Why was Judith surprised by the tall buildings?
  • What questions did Judith ask her mother?

> **PREP NOTE**
> **Setting a Purpose**
> Write questions on a
> chalkboard, white board,
> or large piece of paper
> before working with your
> small group.

3. Reading on Your Own: Partner or Whisper Reading
  • Have students take turns reading every other page with a partner or have students
    whisper read pages 56–59 on their own.
  • Continue having students track each word with their fingers.
  • Have students ask themselves or their partners the gray text questions.

For Whisper Reading, say something like:
Everyone, turn to page 56. This is where you're going to start reading on your own—without
me. You will whisper read as you track with your finger so I can see where you are in your work.
Turn to page 59. That's where you are going to stop reading.
Now turn back to page 56.

For Partner Reading, say something like:
Everyone, turn to page 56. This is where you're going to start Partner Reading.
Where are you going to sit? (at our desks, side by side)
You will take turns reading pages. If you are the listener, what will you do? (keep my book flat,
follow with my finger, compliment my partner)
If you are the reader, what will you do? (keep my book flat, finger track, read quietly)
Turn to page 59. That's where you are going to stop reading.

4. Comprehension and Skill Work

For students on a 6-Day Plan, tell them they will do Comprehension and Skill Activities 1
and 2 after they read on their own. Guide practice, as needed. For teacher directions, see
pages 30 and 31. (For an 8-Day Plan, see the Lesson Planner.)

5. Homework 1: Repeated Reading

ON YOUR OWN

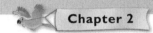

Chapter 2

The Tall Buildings

Isabel knows what will come next in my story. She says, "Mami, were you surprised to see tall buildings?"

I say, "Yes, I was surprised, Isabel. Mexico has many big cities, but I had never been to them. I lived in a small village. The tallest building in the village was our church. It had one floor and a very tall roof, but it was not tall like a city building."

56

JUDITH'S STORY

I tell the children, "Our journey from Mexico was very long. We were crammed into a bus with all our belongings. We kept falling asleep."

I ask Daniel, "How long was our ride?"

He says, "Loooooonnnng." Daniel is very proud of himself because he can help me tell my story too.

"I remember waking up. I looked out the window and could not believe my eyes. I shook my mami. 'Mami, wake up. What is that?' I asked.

"My mami looked out the window and said sleepily, 'What do you mean, Judith?' I remember looking up at the tall buildings. Mami said, 'Oh, those are buildings, Judith.'"

How did Judith and her family get to the United States?**1** What surprised Judith?**2** Why were the tall buildings a surprise?**3** What's the tallest building you've ever seen?**4**

57

COMPREHENDING
AS YOU GO

1 **Remember:** Identifying—How (Judith and her family took the bus to the United States.)

2 **Understand:** Explaining (Judith was surprised by the tall buildings.)

3 **Analyze:** Inferring (Judith was surprised by the tall buildings because there were no tall buildings in her village in Mexico. She had never seen tall buildings before.)

4 **Apply:** Making Connections, Explaining (The hotel downtown is the biggest building around. I went to the top of a skyscraper once . . .)

"'Buildings? Why are they so big?' I asked.

"Mami said, 'Hundreds of people work in the buildings, so they must be big.' I sat quietly thinking about that. The buildings were so tall they looked like they touched the sun.

"Finally, I asked, 'How do people get to the top of the buildings?'

"Mami smiled. 'Ah, they have elevators.'

"I asked, 'What's an elevator?'

"My mother said, 'An elevator is a big box that people get into. It goes up and down. People push buttons so they can get on and off when they want.'

"I asked, 'Can I ride on an elevator?'

"My mother said, 'I will take you and your brother to a tall building, and we will ride in the elevator.'

"I couldn't wait."

When I finish my elevator story, Isabel and Daniel know that it is really time to get ready for bed!

When Judith arrived in the United States, what did she see that was very different from Mexico?[1] What questions did she ask her mother?[2]

58

COMPREHENDING AS YOU GO

❶ **Remember:** Identifying—What (Judith saw very tall buildings.)

❷ **Understand:** Summarizing (Judith asked why the buildings were so big. She asked how people got to the top of the buildings. She asked what an elevator was and if she could ride on one.)

STORY COMPREHENSION

COMPREHENSION PROCESSES

Remember, Understand, Apply

WRITING TRAITS

Conventions—Complete Sentence, Capital, Period
Presentation

Identifying—Narrator

Identifying—What

Identifying—What

Identifying—Why
Using Vocabulary—immigrate

Identifying—What
Using Vocabulary—tradition

Making Connections

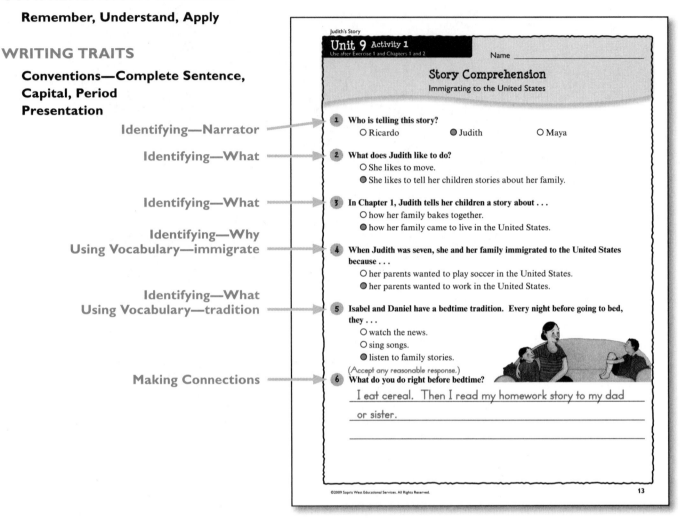

Judith's Story

Unit 9 Activity 1
Use after Exercise 1 and Chapters 1 and 2

Name _____

Story Comprehension
Immigrating to the United States

1. **Who is telling this story?**
   ○ Ricardo   ● Judith   ○ Maya

2. **What does Judith like to do?**
   ○ She likes to move.
   ● She likes to tell her children stories about her family.

3. **In Chapter 1, Judith tells her children a story about . . .**
   ○ how her family bakes together.
   ● how her family came to live in the United States.

4. **When Judith was seven, she and her family immigrated to the United States because . . .**
   ○ her parents wanted to play soccer in the United States.
   ● her parents wanted to work in the United States.

5. **Isabel and Daniel have a bedtime tradition. Every night before going to bed, they . . .**
   ○ watch the news.
   ○ sing songs.
   ● listen to family stories.

(Accept any reasonable response.)
6. **What do you do right before bedtime?**

I eat cereal. Then I read my homework story to my dad
or sister.
_____

©2009 Sopris West Educational Services. All Rights Reserved.   13

PROCEDURES

For each step, demonstrate and guide practice, as needed. Then have students complete the page independently.

1. **Selection Response—Basic Instructions** (Items 1–5)
   • Have students read each sentence stem or question, then fill in the bubble with the correct answer.
   • Think aloud with students and discuss the multiple-choice options, as needed.

2. **Personal Response: Sentence Writing—Specific Instructions** (Item 6)
   • Have students read the question and discuss possible responses.
   • Remind students that all responses are acceptable because everyone has a different bedtime tradition.
   • Have students write two or more complete sentences, using capitals and periods.

Self-monitoring
Have students check and correct their work.

VOCABULARY AND ALPHABETICAL ORDER

COMPREHENSION PROCESSES

Understand, Apply

WRITING TRAITS

Conventions—Period

Alphabetical Order

Defining and Using Vocabulary—
generation; Visualizing; Illustrating

Defining and Using Vocabulary—
immigrate; Visualizing; Illustrating

Defining and Using Vocabulary—
permission; Visualizing; Illustrating

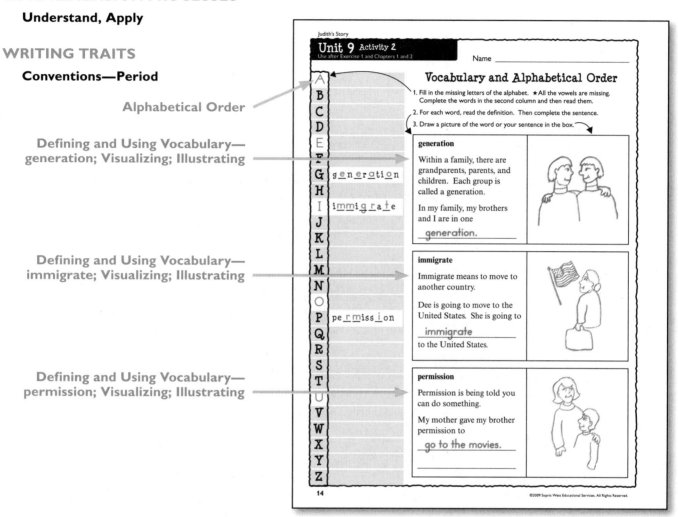

Judith's Story

Unit 9 Activity 2
Use after Exercise 1 and Chapters 1 and 2

Name _____

Vocabulary and Alphabetical Order

1. Fill in the missing letters of the alphabet. ★ All the vowels are missing. Complete the words in the second column and then read them.
2. For each word, read the definition. Then complete the sentence.
3. Draw a picture of the word or your sentence in the box.

generation

Within a family, there are grandparents, parents, and children. Each group is called a generation.

In my family, my brothers and I are in one

generation.

immigrate

Immigrate means to move to another country.

Dee is going to move to the United States. She is going to

immigrate

to the United States.

permission

Permission is being told you can do something.

My mother gave my brother permission to

go to the movies.

14

©2009 Sopris West Educational Services. All Rights Reserved.

PROCEDURES

For each step, demonstrate and guide practice, as needed. Then have students complete the page independently.

Alphabetical Order—Basic Instructions
• Have students read the letters in the alphabet column and fill in the missing letters.
• Have students fill in the blanks for the vocabulary words in the column.

Vocabulary: Sentence Completion, Illustrating—Basic Instructions
• Have students read the vocabulary words and definitions.
• Have students read the sample sentences and fill in the blanks.
• Have students visualize and illustrate each sentence.

Self-monitoring
Have students check and correct their work.

① SOUND REVIEW

Have students read the sounds and key word phrases in each row. Work for accuracy, then fluency.

Read the sounds and the phrases. (/ĪĪĪ/ as in fly, /o͞o/ as in blue, /aw/ as in paw . . .)

② SHIFTY WORD BLENDING

For each word, have students say the underlined sound. Then have them sound out the word smoothly and say it. Use the words in sentences, as appropriate.

③ SOUND PRACTICE

- For each task, have students spell and say the focus sound in the gray bar. For Bossy <u>E</u>, read the header.
- Next, have students read each underlined sound two times, then the word.
  Look at the gray bar. Say <u>o-w</u> says /ōōō/ as in snow. (<u>o-w</u> says /ōōō/ as in snow.)
  Read each sound two times. Then say the word. (/ō/, /ō/, crow; /ō/, /ō/, show; /ō/, /ō/, blow)
- Have students read the whole words in the columns.

④ ACCURACY AND FLUENCY BUILDING

- For each task, have students say any underlined part, then read the word.
- Set a pace. Then have students read the whole words in each task and column.
- Provide repeated practice, building accuracy first, then fluency.

C1. Multisyllabic Words

- For the list of words divided by syllables, have students read and finger count each syllable, then read the whole word. Use the word in a sentence, as appropriate.
- For the list of whole words, build accuracy and then fluency.

surprised	2 syllables	When the dog barked, John was . . . *surprised.*
together	3 syllables	Let's play a game . . . *together.*
Thanksgiving	3 syllables	A holiday for giving thanks is . . . *Thanksgiving.*
immigrated	4 syllables	Mr. Todd moved to the United States. He . . . *immigrated.*
remember	3 syllables	We had a great time. It was an evening to . . . *remember.*
tradition	3 syllables	We travel to my grandparents' house every July. That's our . . . *tradition.*

D1. Tricky Words

- For each Tricky Word, have students use the sounds and word parts they know to silently sound out the word. Use the word in a sentence to help with pronunciation.

worked	Nadia fixed the machine, and it . . . *worked.*
learned	When I got home from school, Mom asked, "What have you . . . *learned?"*
gives	Henry brings an apple to school every day and . . . *gives* . . . it to the teacher.
laughs	When the baby swings high into the air, she . . . *laughs.*

- Have students go back and read the whole words in the column.

⑤ WORDS IN CONTEXT

For each word, have students use the sounds and word parts they know to silently sound out the word. Then have students read the sentence. Assist, as needed.

⑥ **MORPHOGRAPHS AND AFFIXES**
- Have students read each underlined part, then the word.
- Review the morphographs *-ful*, *re-*, and *un-*. Say something like:
  What does *-ful* mean? (full of) So *thankful* means to be full of . . . thanks.
  Continue with "rerun" and "unhappy."

Judith's Story

Unit 9 Exercise 2
Use before Chapter 3

1. SOUND REVIEW Have students review sounds for accuracy, then for fluency.

Ⓐ	-y as in fly	ue as in blue	aw as in paw	ow as in snow	kn as in knee
Ⓑ	ge	ci	o_e	ph	ai

2. SHIFTY WORD BLENDING For each word, have students say the underlined part, sound out smoothly, then read the word.

<u>h</u>ard	h<u>ai</u>r	<u>ch</u>air	<u>ch</u>e<u>er</u>	<u>st</u>eer

3. SOUND PRACTICE In each column, have students spell and say the sound, then say any underlined sound and the word. Next, have students read the whole column.

ow as in snow	-y as in baby	ci, ce	Bossy E
cr<u>ow</u>	cand<u>y</u>	ni<u>ce</u>	gave
sh<u>ow</u>	funn<u>y</u>	pla<u>ce</u>	sp<u>o</u>ke
bl<u>ow</u>	stor<u>y</u>	<u>ci</u>ty	sc<u>a</u>red

4. ACCURACY AND FLUENCY BUILDING For each column, have students say any underlined part, then read each word. Next, have students read the whole column.

A1 Mixed Practice	**B1** Compound Words	**C1** Multisyllabic Words		**D1** Tricky Words
l<u>igh</u>t	classroom	sur·prised	surprised	worked
ab<u>ou</u>t	everyone	to·geth·er	together	learned
bl<u>o</u>nd	sometimes	Thanks·giv·ing	Thanksgiving	gives
d<u>ar</u>k	anyone	im·mi·grat·ed	immigrated	laughs
th<u>i</u>nks		re·mem·ber	remember	
br<u>ow</u>n		tra·di·tion	tradition	

5. WORDS IN CONTEXT For each word, have students use the sounds and word parts they know to figure out the word. Then have them read the sentences.

Ⓐ	ed·u·ca·tion	My mom says I go to school to get an <u>education</u>.
Ⓑ	En·glish	I speak <u>English</u>. Do you?
Ⓒ	an·cient	If something is thousands of years old, it is <u>ancient</u>.

6. MORPHOGRAPHS AND AFFIXES Have students read each underlined part, then the word.

thank<u>ful</u>	<u>re</u>run	<u>e</u>xit	<u>un</u>happy

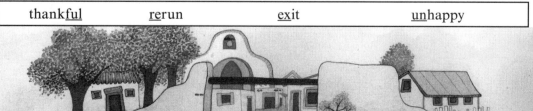

11

33

COMPREHENSION PROCESSES

Remember, Understand

PROCEDURES

Introducing Vocabulary

immigrate, generation

- For each vocabulary word, have students read the word by parts, then read the whole word.
- Read the student-friendly explanations to students as they follow with their fingers. Then have students use the vocabulary word by following the gray text.
- Review and discuss the photos and illustrations.

"The key to a successful vocabulary program is to use both formal and informal encounters so that attention to vocabulary is happening any time and all the time" (McKeown & Beck, p. 21, 2004).

Encourage students to use vocabulary words from *Read Well 2* throughout the day. Here are some suggestions for keeping words alive in your classroom:

Thumbs Up: When a student spontaneously uses a new vocabulary word, give the student a thumbs up.

Vocabulary Stars: Keep a list of vocabulary words on a bulletin board or chart. When you hear a student use a word, put his or her name and a star next to the word.

Rotate words from previous units in and out of practice.

Vocabulary Stars

generation ★Sara ★Nancy
permission ★George ★Matt
drowsy ★Andrew ★Tasha

WITH THE TEACHER

Chapters 3, 4

Vocabulary

im·mi·grate

Immigrate means to move to another country.

Complete this sentence: In this story, Judith and her family . . .**1**

gen·er·a·tion

Within a family, there are grandparents, parents, and children. Each group is called a **generation**.

This is a family tree. What does it show?**2**

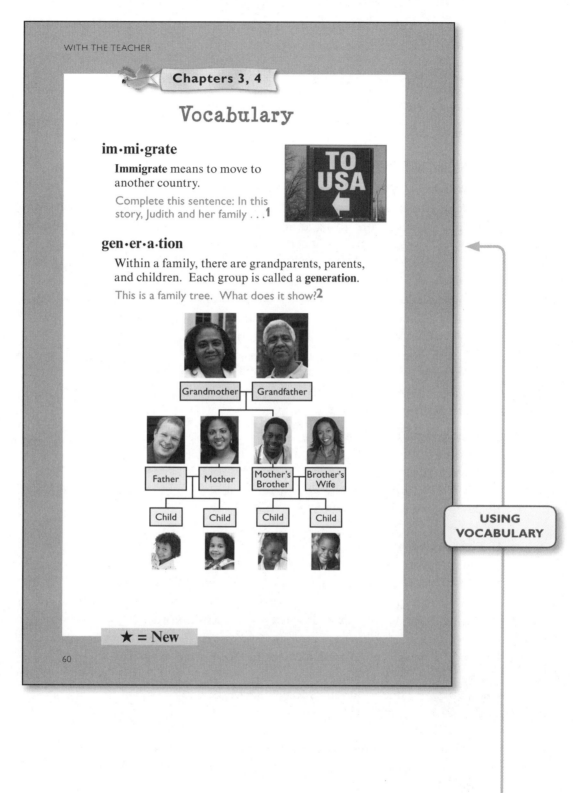

★ = New

60

USING VOCABULARY

❶ Remember: Using Vocabulary—immigrate (immigrated to the United States)

❷ Understand: Explaining; Using Vocabulary—generation (It shows the different generations in the family.)

CHAPTER 3 INSTRUCTIONS
Students read Chapter 3 with the teacher.

COMPREHENSION PROCESSES
Remember, Understand, Apply, Analyze, Create

PROCEDURES

1. Reviewing Chapters 1 and 2

Identifying—Where; Explaining; Summarizing
- Have students turn to page 52. Quickly review how the story started.
- Have students turn to page 56. If time permits, have students reread Chapter 2 with you. Quickly discuss the questions on the board from Setting a Purpose. Say something like:
  Yesterday, you read Chapter 2 on your own. Let's see what you found out.
  Where did Judith live before she moved to the United States? (She lived in a village in Mexico.)
  Why was Judith surprised by the tall buildings?
  (She had never seen a tall building before. Her village did not have tall buildings.)
  What questions did Judith ask her mother?
  (Judith asked, "Why are the buildings so big? How do people get to the top? What is an elevator?" She also asked if she could ride on an elevator.)

2. Introducing Chapter 3

Identifying—Title; Predicting
Introduce the chapter. Say something like:
What's the title of this chapter? (Going to School in America)
What do you think you are going to read about in this story? (We're going to read what it was like for Judith to go to school in America.)

3. First Reading
- Ask questions and discuss the story as indicated by the gray text.
- Mix group and individual turns, independent of your voice.
  Have students work toward a group accuracy goal of 0–4 errors.
- After reading the story, practice any difficult words.

4. Second Reading, Timed Readings: Repeated Reading

- As time allows, have students do Timed Readings while others follow along.
- Time individuals for 30 seconds.

5. Partner or Whisper Reading: Repeated Reading

Before beginning independent work, have students finger track and partner or whisper read.

6. Comprehension and Skill Work
Tell students they will do Comprehension and Skill Activities 3 and 4 after they read Chapter 3. Guide practice, as needed. For teacher directions, see pages 40 and 41.

7. Homework 2: Repeated Reading

JUDITH'S STORY

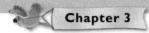

Chapter 3

Going to School in America

Sometimes before bedtime, I tell Isabel and Daniel about first going to school in the United States. I say, "Oh my. The first day Mami took me to school, I remember looking in the classroom. It seemed like everyone had blond hair and blue eyes—even the teacher!"

I tell Isabel and Daniel, "It surprised me to see so many people with blond hair and light skin because everyone in Mexico had dark hair and brown eyes. I was a little scared. I looked different, and I did not speak English."

Why did Judith feel funny her first day of school?[1] If she came to our school, would she feel differently?[2] What would we do to make her feel welcome?[3]

61

NOTE FROM THE AUTHORS
Every immigrant's story is special. Each person's perceptions are unique. The questions on this page were written to help children in diverse communities understand how Judith felt as a new student in a predominantly Anglo-American neighborhood, how it might be the same or different in your community, and how all new students can be made to feel welcome.

COMPREHENDING AS YOU GO

1 Understand: Explaining (She looked different, and she didn't speak English.)

2 Apply: Making Connections, Explaining (Yes. Our school has students from many different backgrounds. There are many African American students, many Hispanic students, and many students who speak different languages.)

3 Create: Generating Ideas (We would tell her our names. We would show her where everything is. We could try to learn her language. We could teach her our language. We could use gestures. We could smile at her. We could play with her. We could give her a special buddy . . .)

Isabel thinks this is funny because her school has many children with dark hair and dark skin and many children with blond hair and light skin too.

"Every day, I went to another room to learn English. My teacher was very nice. She gave candy to us when we worked hard."

Daniel, Isabel, and I always laugh together when I tell this part of my story. Isabel says, "No one ever gives us candy at school!"

I say to Isabel, "This was long ago! After all, I am ancient!"

After we laugh, I tell the children a little more about my education. "In my school, I did learn to speak English, and I made many friends.

"I also learned about a tradition in the United States. I learned about Thanksgiving, and when I was seven, I was thankful for my school. I was thankful to have new friends, and I was thankful that my family immigrated to the United States. I am still thankful for all of those things!"

62

FOCUS ON INFERENCE

Making Connections

After completing the page, say something like:

What was Judith thankful for? (her school, that her family had immigrated, new friends . . .)

Raise your hand if you've gone to a new school. How did you feel after you made new friends?

That's the same way Judith felt. She felt happy and thankful to have made new friends.

JUDITH'S STORY

Think and Talk

EXPLANATION

1. How did Judith feel about her first day of school?

MAKING CONNECTIONS

2. What do we do in our school to help new students feel welcome?

COMPARE/CONTRAST

3. How is your school the same or different from the school Judith went to?

INFERENCE

4. How do you know Judith was glad that she had immigrated to the United States?

63

❶ **Understand:** Explaining (She was a little scared.)

❷ **Apply:** Making Connections, Explaining (We introduce them to the class. We ask another student to be their partner and show them around for a few days . . .)

❸ **Analyze:** Comparing/Contrasting (Our school is different. Almost everyone here has brown hair and brown eyes. Our school is kind of the same because students here go to a different room to learn English too. Our teachers give us stickers, not candy . . .)

❹ **Apply:** Inferring, Explaining (Judith said she was thankful to be in the United States.)

STORY COMPREHENSION

COMPREHENSION PROCESSES

Remember, Apply, Create

WRITING TRAITS

Conventions—Period

Identifying—What

Identifying—What

Making Lists, Making Connections, Generating Ideas

Using Graphic Organizer; Identifying—What; Making Connections

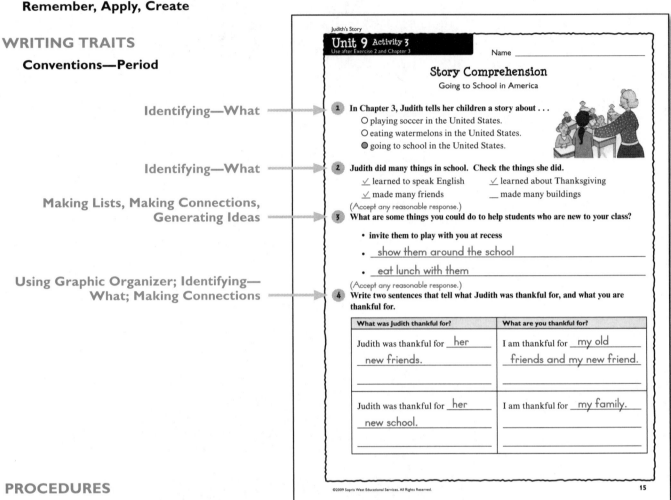

Judith's Story

Unit 9 Activity 3
Use after Exercise 2 and Chapter 3

Name _____

Story Comprehension
Going to School in America

1. In Chapter 3, Judith tells her children a story about . . .
   ○ playing soccer in the United States.
   ○ eating watermelons in the United States.
   ● going to school in the United States.

2. Judith did many things in school. Check the things she did.
   ✓ learned to speak English   ✓ learned about Thanksgiving
   ✓ made many friends   __ made many buildings
   (Accept any reasonable response.)

3. What are some things you could do to help students who are new to your class?
   - invite them to play with you at recess
   - show them around the school
   - eat lunch with them
   (Accept any reasonable response.)

4. Write two sentences that tell what Judith was thankful for, and what you are thankful for.

What was Judith thankful for?	What are you thankful for?
Judith was thankful for _her new friends._	I am thankful for _my old friends and my new friend._
Judith was thankful for _her new school._	I am thankful for _my family._

©2009 Sopris West Educational Services. All Rights Reserved.   15

PROCEDURES

For each step, demonstrate and guide practice, as needed. Then have students complete the page independently.

1. Selection Response—Basic Instructions (Items 1, 2)
   - Have students read each sentence starter, then fill in the bubble or check the blank with the correct answer.
   - Think aloud with students and discuss the multiple-choice options, as needed.

2. Making Lists—Basic Instructions (Item 3)
   - Have students read the question and brainstorm possible answers.
   - Have students write the answers in the blanks.

3. Compare/Contrast: Matrix, Sentence Completion—Basic Instructions (Item 4)
   Have students read the questions and sentence starters. Have them write answers that complete the sentences. Remind students to put a period at the end of each sentence.

Self-monitoring
Have students check and correct their work.

PASSAGE READING FLUENCY

FLUENCY

Accuracy, Expression, Rate

PROCEDURES

For each step, demonstrate and guide practice, as needed. Then have students complete the page independently.

Passage Reading—Basic Instructions

- Have students read the practice words.
- Have students finger track and whisper read the story two times— the first time for accuracy and the second time for expression. Have students cross out a kick ball each time they finish.
- Have students do a one-minute Timed Reading and cross out the timer. Say something like:

You are going to track with your finger and whisper read.

Read the passage three times. The first time, read for accuracy.

What will you read for? (accuracy)

The second time, read for accuracy and expression. What will you read for? (accuracy and expression)

Each time you read, cross out a kick ball and notice how much better your reading sounds.

The last time you read, use the timer. Read quickly but accurately and with expression.

See if you can finish reading before one minute is up.

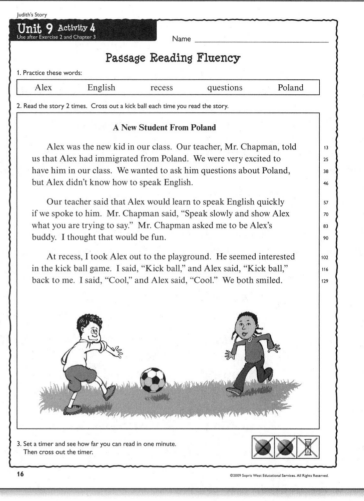

Judith's Story

Unit 9 Activity 4
Use after Exercise 2 and Chapter 3

Name _____

Passage Reading Fluency

1. Practice these words:

| Alex | English | recess | questions | Poland |

2. Read the story 2 times. Cross out a kick ball each time you read the story.

A New Student From Poland

    Alex was the new kid in our class. Our teacher, Mr. Chapman, told us that Alex had immigrated from Poland. We were very excited to have him in our class. We wanted to ask him questions about Poland, but Alex didn't know how to speak English.

    Our teacher said that Alex would learn to speak English quickly if we spoke to him. Mr. Chapman said, "Speak slowly and show Alex what you are trying to say." Mr. Chapman asked me to be Alex's buddy. I thought that would be fun.

    At recess, I took Alex out to the playground. He seemed interested in the kick ball game. I said, "Kick ball," and Alex said, "Kick ball," back to me. I said, "Cool," and Alex said, "Cool." We both smiled.

13
25
38
46

57
70
83
90

102
116
129

3. Set a timer and see how far you can read in one minute. Then cross out the timer.

16

ACCURACY PRECEDES RATE (Reminder)

Students should read the story with a high degree of accuracy before proceeding to Timed Readings. Reading for increased rate before establishing a high degree of accuracy may encourage students to guess at words.

❶ SOUND REVIEW

Use selected Sound Cards from Units 1–8.

❷ ACCURACY AND FLUENCY BUILDING

- For each task, have students say any underlined part, then read the word.
- Set a pace. Then have students read the whole words in each task and column.
- Provide repeated practice, building accuracy first, then fluency.

C1. Word Endings

Have students read any underlined word, then the word with an ending.
Note: Tell students that you change y to i when you add *-er* to "funny" and that you drop the e when you add *-ing* to "come."

D1. Reading by Analogy

Have students figure out how to say "Papi" by reading other words they know.

D2. Compound Words

- Ask students what a compound word is.
- For each word, have students figure out the compound word silently, then read the word.

E1. Tricky Words

- For each Tricky Word, have students use the sounds and word parts they know to silently sound out the word. Use the word in a sentence to help with pronunciation.

laughs	Eden acts silly to get . . . *laughs.*
lived	Some stories begin "Once upon a time, there . . . *lived* . . ."
thought	The teacher asked me what I . . . *thought.*
young	The opposite of old is . . . *young.*
beautiful	The flower garden is . . . *beautiful.*
million	Cynthia worked hard and made a . . . *million* . . . dollars.

- Have students go back and read the whole words in the column.

❸ WORDS IN CONTEXT

For each word, have students use the sounds and word parts they know to silently sound out the word. Then have students read the sentence. Assist, as needed.

❹ MULTISYLLABIC WORDS

For each word, have students read the syllables, then the whole word. Use the word in a sentence, as appropriate. For Row B, have students read each whole word.

remember	Danny didn't know. He couldn't . . . *remember.*
giggles	Whenever Sabra is tickled, she . . . *giggles.*
children	My classroom is full of smart . . . *children.*
different	They weren't the same. They were . . . *different.*
family	My brothers, sisters, and parents are my . . . *family.*
dollars	Neil made a million . . . *dollars.*

⑤ **MORPHOGRAPHS AND AFFIXES**
- Have students read the underlined part, then the word.
- Repeat practice with whole words, mixing group and individual turns. Build accuracy, then fluency.

Judith's Story

Unit 9 Exercise 3
Use before Chapter 4

1. SOUND REVIEW Use selected Sound Cards from Units 1–8.

2. ACCURACY AND FLUENCY BUILDING For each column, have students say any underlined part, then read each word. Next, have students read the whole column.

A1 Mixed Practice	B1 Related Words	C1 Word Endings	D1 Reading by Analogy	E1 Tricky Words
lawns	immigrate	houses	mommy	laughs
mow	immigrant	jobs	Mami	lived
story	immigrants	yards	Papi	thought
know	immigrated			young
village		funny	**D2** Compound Words	beautiful
A2 Bossy E	teach	funnier	someday	million
tile	teacher	come	understand	
nice	teachers	coming	himself	
smile				

3. WORDS IN CONTEXT For each word, have students use the sounds and word parts they know to figure out the word. Then have them read the sentence.

Ⓐ	i•ma•gine	Pretend you are a bird and imagine flying in the sky.
Ⓑ	ed•u•ca•tion	I go to school to get a good education.

4. MULTISYLLABIC WORDS Have students read each word part, then read each whole word. For Row B, have students read each whole word.

Ⓐ	re•mem•ber	remember	gig•gles	giggles
Ⓑ	children	different	family	dollars

5. MORPHOGRAPHS AND AFFIXES Have students read each underlined part, then the word.

Ⓐ	wonderful	action	lovely	thankful
Ⓑ	untrue	explain	noticeable	before

CHAPTER 4 INSTRUCTIONS
Students read Chapter 4 with the teacher.

COMPREHENSION PROCESSES
Remember, Understand, Apply, Analyze, Evaluate

PROCEDURES

1. Reviewing Chapters 1–3

Identifying—Main Character, Narrator; Explaining; Summarizing
Have students identify the main character and what happened in Chapters 1–3.
In Chapters 1 and 2, you met the main character. Who is the main character?
(Judith is the main character.)
Who is the narrator of the story? (Judith is the narrator.)
How did the story begin? (The story began with Judith moving, or immigrating, to the United States.)
In Chapter 2, we found out what surprised Judith the most when she arrived in the United States. What was she surprised by? (She was surprised by the tall buildings.)
What was one of the things she most wanted to do? (She wanted to ride in an elevator.)
In Chapter 3, Judith ended the chapter by telling what she was thankful for. What were some of those things? (She was thankful for new friends, learning English, her school, immigrating to the United States . . .)

2. Introducing Chapter 4

Identifying—Title; Predicting
Have students identify the title and predict what Judith will tell about next.
What's the title of this chapter? (Lovely Green Lawns)
Look at the pictures. What do you think Judith is going to tell us about in this chapter?

3. First Reading
- Ask questions and discuss the text as indicated by the gray text.
- Mix group and individual turns, independent of your voice.
  Have students work toward a group accuracy goal of 0–4 errors.
- After reading the story, practice any difficult words.

4. Second Reading, Short Passage Practice: Developing Prosody
- Demonstrate expressive, fluent reading of the first two paragraphs.
- Guide practice with your voice.
- Provide individual turns while others track with their fingers and whisper read.
- Repeat with one paragraph or page at a time.

5. Partner or Whisper Reading: Repeated Reading

Before beginning independent work, have students finger track and partner or whisper read.

6. Comprehension and Skill Work
Tell students they will do Comprehension and Skill Activities 5 and 6 after they read Chapter 4. Guide practice, as needed. For teacher directions, see pages 50 and 51.

> **PACING**
> **(Reminder)**
> When demonstrating, read at a rate just slightly faster than students' rate.

> **CORRECTING DECODING ERRORS**
> During story reading, gently correct any error, then have students reread the sentence.

7. Homework 3: Repeated Reading

WITH THE TEACHER

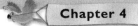

Chapter 4

Lovely Green Lawns

One night, I say to the children, "I think you are ready to hear about the lovely green lawns."

The children look at me. "Lawns?" asks Isabel. "Is it a funny story?"

I say, "Yes, it is funny, because the one thing I remember the most about coming to the United States is the lawns."

64

COMPREHENSION BUILDING (Reminder)

Encourage students to answer questions with complete sentences. If students have difficulty comprehending, think aloud with them or reread the portion of the story that answers the question. Then repeat the question.

JUDITH'S STORY

Isabel says, "I think that is a very funny thing to remember."

I explain, "Where I lived in Mexico, the houses were very small and there were no yards. The houses had dirt and sometimes tile around them. My small country village was so different. Before I came to the United States, I had never seen a lawn. Imagine that!"

Isabel giggles, so Daniel giggles too. I say, "A lawn is a beautiful thing!"

Why did Judith think a lawn was so beautiful? **1**

65

COMPREHENDING
AS YOU GO

1 Understand: Explaining, Comparing/Contrasting (In Mexico, they didn't have lawns. The houses had dirt and tile around them. Judith had never seen a lawn before, so lawns were especially beautiful.)

I say to the children, "Oh my, this story is funnier than I thought it would be."

I ask, "Do you know what my dream was?"

Isabel says, "A million dollars?"

I say, "Oh no. When I came to the United States, my dream was to have a nice house, a lovely green lawn, and a good education. This was my dream."

When I say this, Isabel and Daniel smile. I wonder if they are too young to understand, but Isabel says, "I have a nice house."

Then Daniel says, "Me too."

Then Isabel says, "We have a green lawn too, but we have to mow the lawn."

At that, Ricardo laughs. We all laugh!

We hug the kids and put them to bed. Someday I will tell the children how Ricardo and I got our house and green lawn.

66

JUDITH'S STORY

But for now, I will tell you. My mami and papi said I should work hard in school. That is what I did. That is what Ricardo did too. We got a very good education and good jobs. We help teachers work with children who are immigrants. We also have a wonderful family. I have much to be thankful for!

Why do you think Judith feels so lucky?[1]

67

FOCUS ON CONCLUSIONS

Inferring, Responding

After completing the page, say something like:
The book tells you what Judith's dream was. What was her dream? (Her dream was a good education, a nice house, and a green lawn.)

What does Judith have now? (She has a fine house with a colorful garden.)

The book doesn't say, but how did Judith get her dream? There is a clue in the book. Who can find the clue? (It says she worked hard in school.)

It also says she and Ricardo both work in schools. The book doesn't say, but how do you think Judith feels about her work with immigrant children?

I think Judith is very happy. What do you think?

COMPREHENDING AS YOU GO

❶ **Apply:** Inferring, Explaining (She got a good education. She has a good job and a wonderful family . . .)

COMPREHENSION BUILDING: ORAL STORY RETELL

COMPREHENSION PROCESSES

Remember, Understand

PROCEDURES

◆◆ ELL students and students with language delays will benefit from the oral story retell. Students with strong English oral language skills can skip this activity.

Have students study the pictures, then ask questions and discuss the pictures as indicated by the gray text. The circle, square, and triangle provide visual references for the beginning, middle, and end of the story.

WITH THE TEACHER

Story Retell

JUDITH'S STORY

We're going to retell Judith's story.
Who is the narrator?**1**

● At the beginning of the story, what did you learn about Judith? Use the word *immigrated*.**2**

■ What happened in the middle of the story after Judith and her family arrived in the United States?**3**

▲ What did you learn at the end of Judith's story? **4**

68

---

❶ **Remember:** Identifying—Narrator, Main Character (Judith is the narrator. Judith is also the main character.)

❷ **Remember:** Identifying—Beginning; Using Vocabulary—immigrate (Judith immigrated to the United States when she was seven. When she first came to the United States, she was surprised by the tall buildings.)

❸ **Understand:** Summarizing—Middle, Action (Judith went to a new school. At first she was nervous. She learned English. She made many friends. She got a good education.)

❹ **Understand:** Explaining—End (Judith worked hard in school, got a good education, and a good job. She is happy and thankful for all that she has—including her family.)

◆◆ = Repeat and extend practice for English Language Learners and students with language delays.

MAZE READING AND VISUALIZATION • FOLLOWING DIRECTIONS

COMPREHENSION PROCESSES

Understand

Comprehension Monitoring, Test Taking

Following Directions, Illustrating

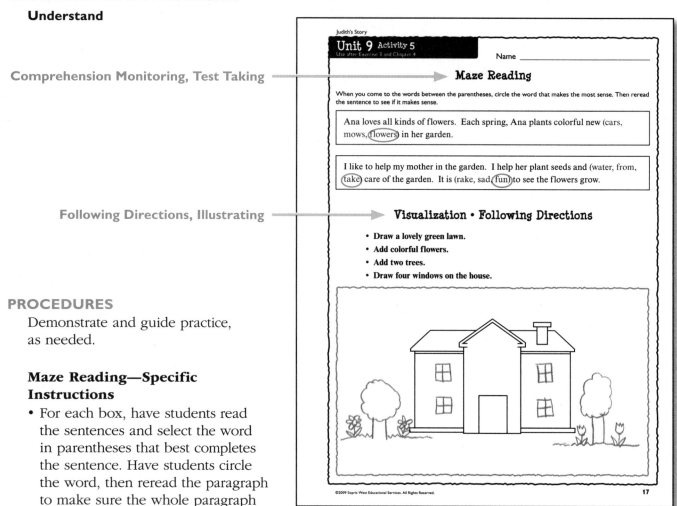

Judith's Story

Unit 9 Activity 5
Use after Exercise 3 and Chapter 4

Name _____

Maze Reading

When you come to the words between the parentheses, circle the word that makes the most sense. Then reread the sentence to see if it makes sense.

Ana loves all kinds of flowers. Each spring, Ana plants colorful new (cars, mows, (flowers)) in her garden.

I like to help my mother in the garden. I help her plant seeds and (water, from, (take)) care of the garden. It is (rake, sad, (fun)) to see the flowers grow.

Visualization • Following Directions

- Draw a lovely green lawn.
- Add colorful flowers.
- Add two trees.
- Draw four windows on the house.

©2009 Sopris West Educational Services. All Rights Reserved.   17

PROCEDURES

Demonstrate and guide practice, as needed.

Maze Reading—Specific Instructions

- For each box, have students read the sentences and select the word in parentheses that best completes the sentence. Have students circle the word, then reread the paragraph to make sure the whole paragraph makes sense. Say something like:

Remember, a maze is like a puzzle. You will choose the correct word to complete the sentence.

Let's read the sentences in the first box. Read and stop at the parentheses.

(Ana loves all kinds of flowers. Each spring, Ana plants colorful new . . .)

There are three choices. Let's try reading the whole sentence with the first choice.

Each spring, Ana plants colorful new . . . *cars* . . . in her garden.

Does that word choice make sense? (no)

No. It's funny, but it doesn't make sense. Let's try the next word. Each spring, Ana plants colorful new . . . *mows* . . . in her garden.

Does that make sense? (no)

Let's try the last word. Each spring, Ana plants colorful new . . . *flowers* . . . in her garden.

Does that make sense? (yes) So that word is the best. Circle that word.

Read the whole box. (Ana loves all kinds of flowers. Each spring, Ana plants colorful new flowers in her garden.)

- Repeat with the next box.

Visualizing, Following Directions—Basic Instructions

Have students read the directions, visualize, then add details to the picture, as instructed.

MAIN IDEA AND SUPPORTING DETAILS

COMPREHENSION PROCESSES
Remember, Understand, Apply

WRITING TRAITS
Conventions—Complete Sentence, Beginning Capital, Period

Identifying—Who

Using Graphic Organizer; Identifying—Supporting Details, Main Idea Sentence Writing Sentence Completion

Visualizing, Illustrating

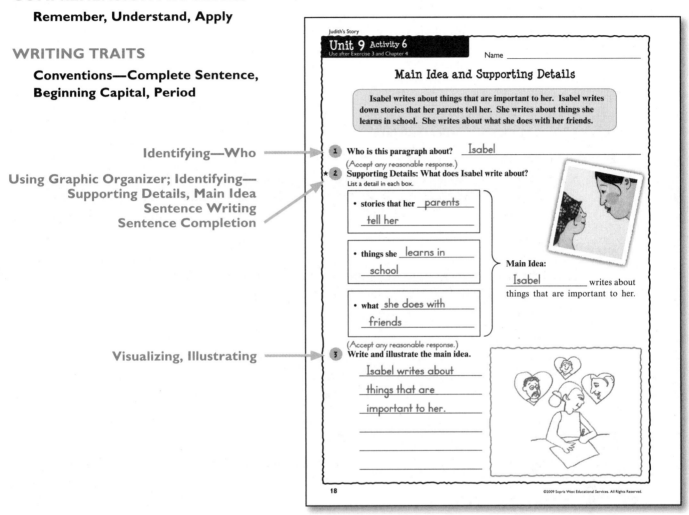

Judith's Story

Unit 9 Activity 6
Use after Exercise 3 and Chapter 4

Name _____

Main Idea and Supporting Details

Isabel writes about things that are important to her. Isabel writes down stories that her parents tell her. She writes about things she learns in school. She writes about what she does with her friends.

1 Who is this paragraph about? _Isabel_

(Accept any reasonable response.)
★2 Supporting Details: What does Isabel write about?
List a detail in each box.

- stories that her _parents_ _tell her_

- things she _learns in_ _school_

- what _she does with_ _friends_

Main Idea:
Isabel writes about things that are important to her.

(Accept any reasonable response.)
3 Write and illustrate the main idea.
Isabel writes about
things that are
important to her.

18   ©2009 Sopris West Educational Services. All Rights Reserved.

PROCEDURES

For each step, demonstrate and guide practice, as needed. Then have students complete the page independently.

1. Topic/Who: Answering Questions—Basic Instructions (Item 1)
- Have students read the top paragraph.
- Have students read the question and write the correct answer in the blank.

2. Main Idea/Supporting Details: Hierarchy Chart—Basic Instructions (Item 2)
- Have students read the question, then fill in the blanks to complete the supporting details.
- Have students fill in the blank to complete the main idea.

3. Main Idea: Sentence Writing, Illustrating—Basic Instructions (Item 3)
Have students write the main idea sentence. Remind them to use a capital and a period. Then have students draw a picture of the main idea.

1 SOUND REVIEW

Have students read the sounds and key word phrases. Work for accuracy, then fluency.

2 ACCURACY AND FLUENCY BUILDING

- For each task, have students say any underlined part, then read the word.
- Set a pace. Then have students read the whole words in each task and column.
- Provide repeated practice, building accuracy first, then fluency.

D1. Possessives

- Tell students that words with an apostrophe <u>s</u> show ownership.
- Have students read each word.

E1. Tricky Words

- For each Tricky Word, have students use the sounds and word parts they know to silently sound out the word. Use the word in a sentence to help with pronunciation.
- If the word is unfamiliar, tell students the word. Then have students say, spell, and say it.

toward

Look at the first word. Sound the word out in your head. When you think you know it, thumbs up. Say the word with me. toward Spell the word. (<u>t</u>-<u>o</u>-<u>w</u>-<u>a</u>-<u>r</u>-<u>d</u>)
Yule headed for home. He headed . . . *toward* . . . home.
Read the word three times. (toward, toward, toward)

favorite

Look at the next word. Say the word parts with me. fav-or-ite
The one you like best is your . . . *favorite.*
Read the word three times. (favorite, favorite, favorite)

| **walk** | I missed the bus, so I had to . . . *walk.* |
| **laugh** | She was so happy, she had to . . . *laugh.* |

- Have students go back and read the whole words in the column.

3 MULTISYLLABIC WORDS

For each word, have students read each syllable, finger count, and then read the whole word. Use the word in a sentence, as appropriate.

chuckling	2 syllables	He was laughing quietly. He was . . . *chuckling.*
ruckus	2 syllables	When the fox got into the henhouse, there was a big . . . *ruckus.*
glisten	2 syllables	The sun shining on the water made it . . . *glisten.*
chickens	2 syllables	On our farm, we have horses, sheep, and . . . *chickens.*

4 WORDS IN CONTEXT

For each word, have students use the sounds and word parts they know to silently sound out the word. Then have students read the sentence. Assist, as needed.

5 MORPHOGRAPHS AND AFFIXES

Ricardo's Stories

Unit 9 Exercise 4
Use before Chapter 1

1. SOUND REVIEW Have students review sounds for accuracy, then for fluency.

A	OW as in cow	igh as in flight	i_e as in kite	ar as in star	ch as in chicken
B	ay	ce	ir	ew	u_e

2. ACCURACY AND FLUENCY BUILDING For each column, have students say any underlined part, then read each word. Next, have students read the whole column.

A1 Mixed Practice	**B1** Bossy E	**C1** Word Endings	**D1** Possessives	**E1** Tricky Words
sh<u>oo</u>	l<u>i</u>ke	<u>fr</u>y<u>ing</u>	Grandmother's	toward
f<u>ew</u>	sm<u>i</u>le	<u>miss</u>ed	Daniel's	favorite
b<u>or</u>n	m<u>a</u>kes	h<u>ouse</u>s	Judith's	walk
gr<u>ow</u>ing	r<u>a</u>ce		**D2** Compound Words	laugh
gr<u>a</u>b	<u>u</u>sed	story	whenever	
cl<u>ue</u>		stories	grandmother	
h<u>igh</u>			doorway	
<u>a</u>lways		try		
y<u>e</u>ll		tried		

3. MULTISYLLABIC WORDS Have students read and finger count each word part, then read each whole word.

A	chuck•ling	chuckling	ruck•us	ruckus
B	glis•ten	glisten	chick•ens	chickens

4. WORDS IN CONTEXT For each word, have students use the sounds and word parts they know to figure out the word. Then have them read the sentence.

A	wan•dered	"Moo," said the lost cow as she <u>wandered</u> around.
B	hus•band	John White is Mrs. White's <u>husband</u>.
C	ho•la (oh-lah)	The Spanish word for hello is <u>hola</u>.

5. MORPHOGRAPHS AND AFFIXES Have students read each underlined word part, then the word.

<u>bi</u>fold	slow<u>ly</u>	<u>ex</u>it	<u>o</u>pened	<u>re</u>write

COMPREHENSION PROCESSES
Remember, Understand

PROCEDURES

1. Introducing the Story

Using Table of Contents; Identifying—Title, Who; Predicting

Find the Table of Contents. What page is it on?　(page 2)

Yes, pages 2 and 3 show what's in Unit 8. Now turn to pages 4 and 5.
Touch the title of Unit 9. What's the title of this unit?　(Family Tales)

Find the second story in Unit 9. What is it called?
(Ricardo's Stories)
On what page does "Ricardo's Stories" start?　(page 69)
That's right. Everyone, turn to page 69.

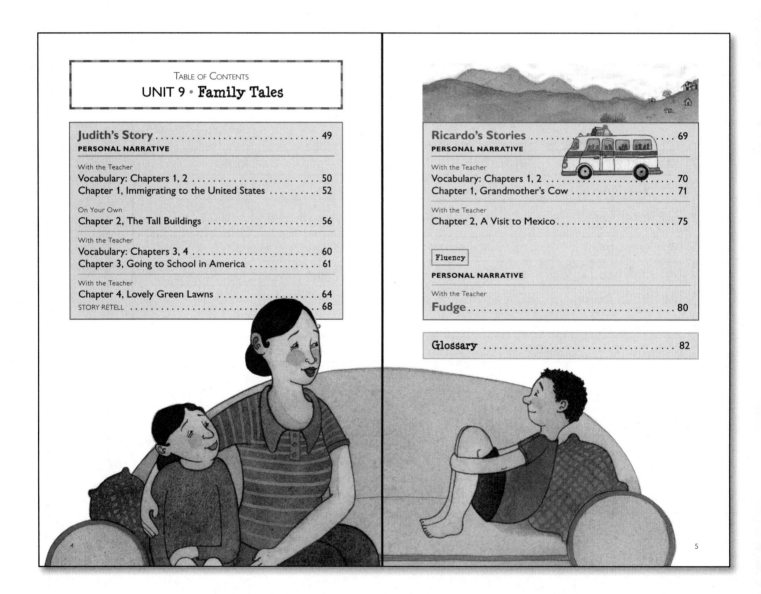

TABLE OF CONTENTS
UNIT 9 • Family Tales

Judith's Story 49
PERSONAL NARRATIVE

With the Teacher
Vocabulary: Chapters 1, 2 50
Chapter 1, Immigrating to the United States 52

On Your Own
Chapter 2, The Tall Buildings 56

With the Teacher
Vocabulary: Chapters 3, 4 60
Chapter 3, Going to School in America 61

With the Teacher
Chapter 4, Lovely Green Lawns 64
STORY RETELL 68

Ricardo's Stories 69
PERSONAL NARRATIVE

With the Teacher
Vocabulary: Chapters 1, 2 70
Chapter 1, Grandmother's Cow 71

With the Teacher
Chapter 2, A Visit to Mexico 75

Fluency

PERSONAL NARRATIVE

With the Teacher
Fudge 80

Glossary 82

2. Introducing the Title Page

Inferring; Identifying—Title, Who, Illustrator; Predicting

- Have students identify the story title. Say something like:

  Everyone, touch the title of our new story. What's the title of this story? (Ricardo's Stories)

  Does anyone remember who Ricardo is? (Ricardo is Judith's husband.)

  That's right. Judith told us that her husband was named Ricardo.

- Read the gray text at the bottom of page 69. Then say something like:

  What do you think Ricardo's stories are about?

  (Maybe they are about Ricardo immigrating to the United States. Maybe he will tell us about growing up in Mexico . . .)

- Have students look at the drawing on page 69. Explain to students that this is a drawing of Ricardo. Say something like:

  Look at the picture on page 69. That is a drawing of Ricardo. Who do you think drew this picture of Ricardo? (Johanna Van Der Sterre)

  That's right. It says that this story was illustrated by Johanna Van Der Sterre.

  That means Johanna Van Der Sterre drew the pictures.

Ricardo's Stories

a personal narrative
by Ricardo Peinado, Ph.D.
illustrated by Johanna Van Der Sterre

From generation to generation, families grow and experience new things. Every family and every family member has his or her own stories to tell. These are a few of Ricardo's own stories. He is happy to share his stories with you.

69

COMPREHENSION PROCESSES

Understand, Apply

PROCEDURES

Introducing Vocabulary

> **generation, permission** ☆ **glisten** ☆ **drowsy**

- For each vocabulary word, have students read the word by parts, then read the whole word.
- Read the student-friendly explanations to students as they follow with their fingers. Then have students use the vocabulary word by following the gray text.
- Review and discuss the photos and illustrations.

☆ = New in this unit

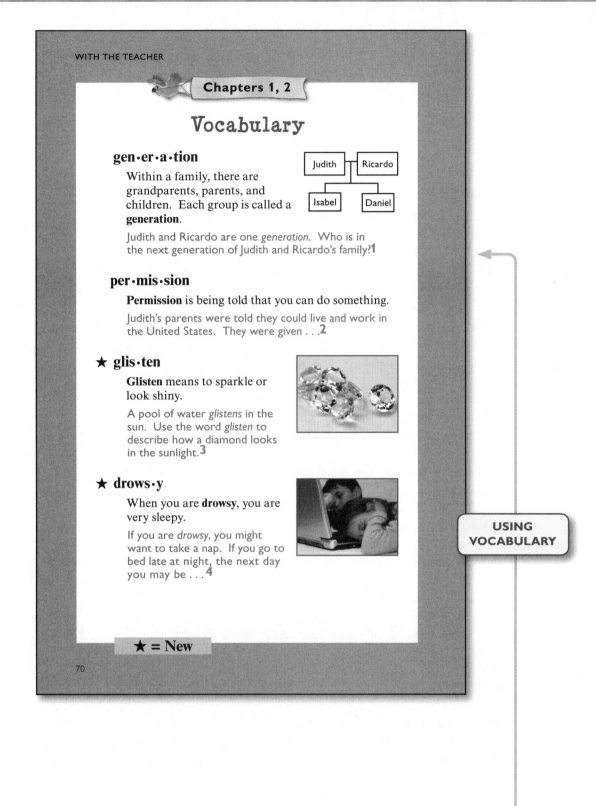

WITH THE TEACHER

Chapters 1, 2

Vocabulary

gen·er·a·tion

Within a family, there are grandparents, parents, and children. Each group is called a **generation**.

Judith	Ricardo
Isabel	Daniel

Judith and Ricardo are one *generation*. Who is in the next generation of Judith and Ricardo's family?**1**

per·mis·sion

Permission is being told that you can do something.

Judith's parents were told they could live and work in the United States. They were given . . .**2**

★ glis·ten

Glisten means to sparkle or look shiny.

A pool of water *glistens* in the sun. Use the word *glisten* to describe how a diamond looks in the sunlight.**3**

★ drows·y

When you are **drowsy**, you are very sleepy.

If you are *drowsy*, you might want to take a nap. If you go to bed late at night, the next day you may be . . .**4**

★ = New

70

USING VOCABULARY

❶ **Apply:** Using Vocabulary—generation (Their children, Isabel and Daniel, are the next generation.)

❷ **Understand:** Using Vocabulary—permission (permission)

❸ **Understand:** Using Vocabulary—glisten (A diamond glistens in the sunlight.)

❹ **Understand:** Using Vocabulary—drowsy (drowsy)

CHAPTER 1 INSTRUCTIONS
Students read Chapter 1 with the teacher.

COMPREHENSION PROCESSES
Remember, Understand, Apply, Analyze, Evaluate

PROCEDURES

1. Introducing Chapter 1

Identifying—Title; Predicting
Discuss the title. Ask students what they think the first chapter will
be about.
Say something like:
Read the title of the chapter. (Grandmother's Cow)
Who do you think this chapter will be about? (Grandmother and a cow)

2. First Reading
- Ask questions and discuss the story as indicated by the gray text.
- Mix group and individual turns, independent of your voice.
  Have students work toward a group accuracy goal of 0–4 errors.
  Quietly keep track of errors made by all students in the group.
- After reading the story, practice any difficult words.
  Reread the story if students have not reached the accuracy goal.

3. Second Reading, Timed Readings: Repeated Reading
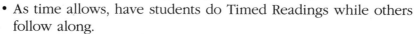
- As time allows, have students do Timed Readings while others
  follow along.
- Time individuals for 30 seconds, and encourage each child to
  work for a personal best.
- Count the number of words read correctly in 30 seconds (words read
  minus errors). Multiply by two to determine words correct per minute.
  Record student scores.

4. Partner or Whisper Reading: Repeated Reading

Before beginning independent work, have students finger track
and partner or whisper read.

5. Comprehension and Skill Work
Tell students they will do Comprehension and Skill Activities 7 and 8 after
they read Chapter 1. Guide practice, as needed. For teacher directions, see
pages 63 and 64.

6. Homework 4: Repeated Reading

**TIME
MANAGEMENT
NOTE**
You may now wish to
begin assessing the highest
performers in your group.

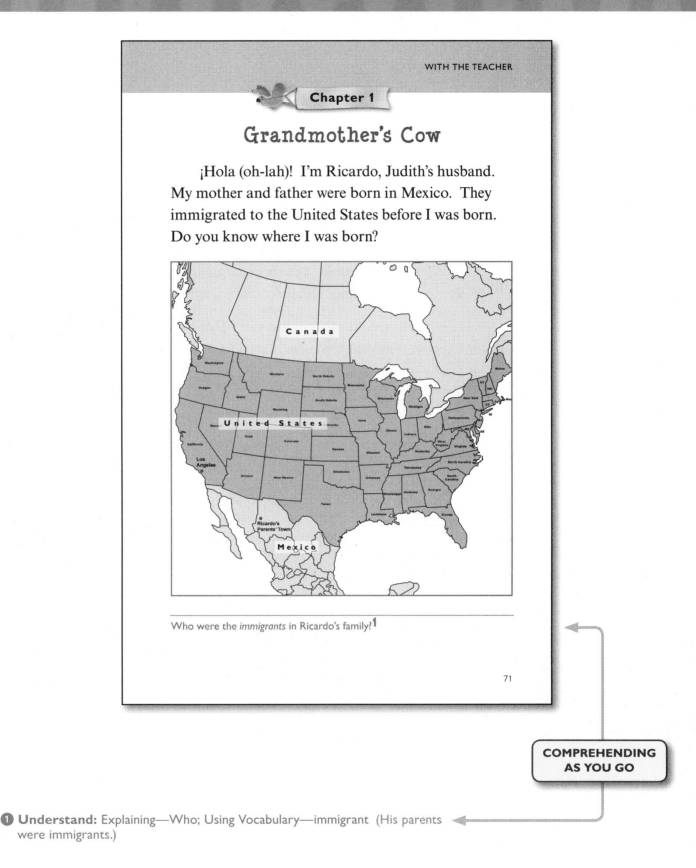

WITH THE TEACHER

Chapter 1

Grandmother's Cow

¡Hola (oh-lah)! I'm Ricardo, Judith's husband. My mother and father were born in Mexico. They immigrated to the United States before I was born. Do you know where I was born?

Who were the *immigrants* in Ricardo's family?[1]

71

COMPREHENDING AS YOU GO

❶ **Understand:** Explaining—Who; Using Vocabulary—immigrant (His parents were immigrants.)

WITH THE TEACHER

I would like to tell you my favorite story. It is one of Isabel and Daniel's favorite stories too. It is about an old cow and my grandmother.

My mother used to tell this story. She always started by saying, "In Mexico, when I was growing up, we had chickens and a few cows that just wandered around our houses."

Think about that! The animals could go wherever they wanted, whenever they wanted.

Mama would chuckle and say, "There was an old cow. That old cow always tried to come into your grandmother's house, but she would shoo it out. You should have seen Grandmother when that old cow showed up in the doorway.

"Grandmother would grab her frying pan and run toward the cow saying, 'Out, out, out.'

"Then the old cow would go, 'Moooo.' But she would not move.

"This would make Grandmother yell, 'Go, go, go,' until the cow finally moved."

Who told Ricardo this story?**1** Where did the story take place?**2** Why did Ricardo's mother chuckle when she told him this story?**3**

72

COMPREHENDING AS YOU GO

❶ Remember: Identifying—Who (His mother told him the story.)

❷ Remember: Identifying—Setting (The story took place in Mexico.)

❸ Apply: Inferring, Explaining (She thought it was funny that her mother would run after a cow with a frying pan . . .)

RICARDO'S STORIES

My mother would end the story by chuckling and saying, "Oh, what a ruckus! After a while, the old cow would slowly walk off."

What do you think a ruckus is? [1] Do you think the story is funny? Why or why not? [2] Do you think Ricardo's grandmother lived in the country or in a city? [3]

73

COMPREHENDING AS YOU GO

❶ **Apply:** Inferring; Explaining; Using Vocabulary—commotion (A ruckus is a lot of noise. A ruckus is like a commotion . . .)

❷ **Evaluate:** Responding (I think the story is funny because the grandmother chased the cow with a frying pan. It would be funnier if the cow chased the grandmother . . .)

❸ **Apply:** Inferring, Explaining (She lived in the country where the animals could wander around.)

WITH THE TEACHER

Daniel and Isabel like this story. It makes them laugh just like I laughed when my mother told me the story.

Whenever my mother talked about growing up in Mexico, she would smile and her eyes would glisten. But then she would look a little sad too. I think my mother missed Mexico.

INFERENCE

1. Why do you think Daniel and Isabel laugh when Ricardo tells this story?

INFERENCE

2. What makes this story funny?

DRAWING CONCLUSIONS

3. Ricardo's mother would smile but her eyes would glisten. Why would Ricardo's mother's eyes glisten?

INFERENCE

4. What makes this story bittersweet?

74

❶ **Apply:** Inferring, Explaining (They think the story is funny.)

❷ **Apply:** Inferring, Explaining (It's funny to think about a grandmother chasing a cow with a frying pan.)

❸ **Analyze:** Drawing Conclusions; **Apply:** Using Vocabulary—glisten (She was sad too. When you're sad, you get tears in your eyes. The tears glisten.)

❹ **Apply:** Inferring; Explaining; Using Vocabulary—bittersweet (It's bittersweet because it is both happy and sad. Ricardo's mother is happy to be in the United States, but she also misses Mexico and her family in Mexico.)

STORY COMPREHENSION

COMPREHENSION PROCESSES

Remember, Understand

WRITING TRAITS

Conventions—Period

Identifying—Who

Identifying—What

Identifying—Setting

Identifying—What

Identifying—What

Identifying—What

Defining and Using Vocabulary—
bittersweet

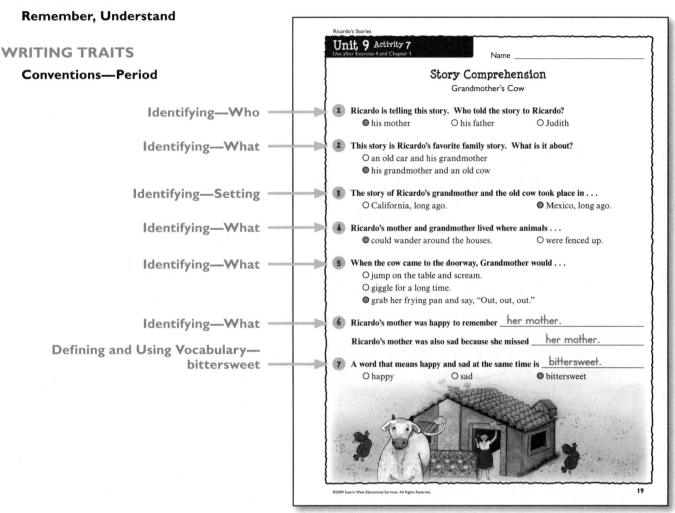

Ricardo's Stories

Unit 9 Activity 7
Use after Exercise 4 and Chapter 1

Name _____

Story Comprehension
Grandmother's Cow

1. Ricardo is telling this story. Who told the story to Ricardo?
   ● his mother   ○ his father   ○ Judith

2. This story is Ricardo's favorite family story. What is it about?
   ○ an old car and his grandmother
   ● his grandmother and an old cow

3. The story of Ricardo's grandmother and the old cow took place in . . .
   ○ California, long ago.   ● Mexico, long ago.

4. Ricardo's mother and grandmother lived where animals . . .
   ● could wander around the houses.   ○ were fenced up.

5. When the cow came to the doorway, Grandmother would . . .
   ○ jump on the table and scream.
   ○ giggle for a long time.
   ● grab her frying pan and say, "Out, out, out."

6. Ricardo's mother was happy to remember __her mother.__

   Ricardo's mother was also sad because she missed __her mother.__

7. A word that means happy and sad at the same time is __bittersweet.__
   ○ happy   ○ sad   ● bittersweet

19

PROCEDURES

For each step, demonstrate and guide practice, as needed. Then have students complete the page independently.

Selection Response—Basic Instructions (Items 1–7)

- Have students read each sentence or question, then fill in the bubble and/or blank with the correct answer.
- Think aloud with students and discuss the multiple-choice options, as needed.
- Remind students to end sentences with a period, where needed.

Self-monitoring

Have students check and correct their work.

MAIN IDEA AND SUPPORTING DETAILS

COMPREHENSION PROCESSES

Remember, Understand, Apply

WRITING TRAITS

Conventions—Complete Sentence, Capital, Period

PROCEDURES

For each step, demonstrate and guide practice, as needed. Then have students complete the page independently.

1. **Topic/Who: Answering Questions—Basic Instructions** (Item 1)
   - Have students read the top paragraph.
   - Have students read the question and write the correct answer in the blank.

2. **Main Idea/Supporting Details: Hierarchy Chart—Basic Instructions** (Item 2)
   - Have students read the question, then fill in the blanks to complete the supporting details.
   - Have students fill in the blank to complete the main idea.

3. **Main Idea: Sentence Writing, Illustrating—Basic Instructions** (Item 3)
   Have students write the main idea sentence. Remind them to use a capital and a period. Then have students draw a picture of the main idea.

Identifying—
Main Character

Using Graphic
Organizer
Identifying—
Supporting Details,
Main Idea
Sentence Completion
Sentence Writing

Inferring—Main Idea
Illustrating

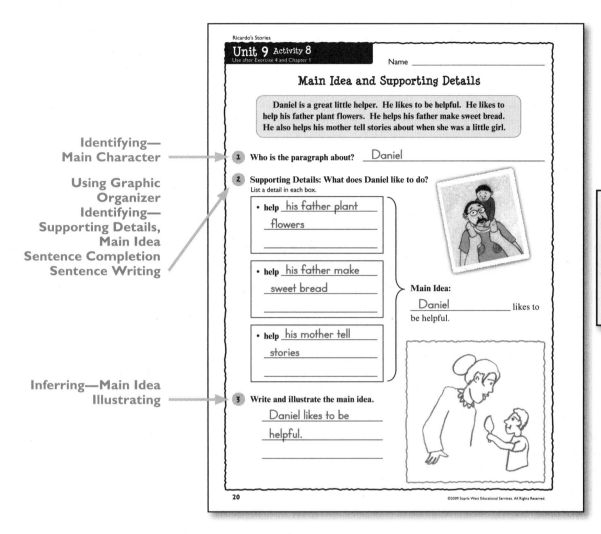

Ricardo's Stories

Unit 9 Activity 8
Use after Exercise 4 and Chapter 1

Name _____

Main Idea and Supporting Details

> Daniel is a great little helper. He likes to be helpful. He likes to help his father plant flowers. He helps his father make sweet bread. He also helps his mother tell stories about when she was a little girl.

1 Who is the paragraph about? _Daniel_

2 Supporting Details: What does Daniel like to do?
List a detail in each box.

- help _his father plant flowers_
- help _his father make sweet bread_
- help _his mother tell stories_

Main Idea:
Daniel likes to be helpful.

3 Write and illustrate the main idea.
Daniel likes to be helpful.

20   ©2009 Sopris West Educational Services. All Rights Reserved.

CHECKOUT OPPORTUNITY

Listen to your students read individually while others work. When possible, provide your lowest-performing students with one-to-one practice.

① SOUND REVIEW

Use selected Sound Cards from Units 1–8.

PACING

Exercise 5a should take about 10 minutes, allowing about 10 minutes for the Personal Narrative Focus Lesson.

② ACCURACY AND FLUENCY BUILDING

- For each task, have students say any underlined part, then read the word.
- Set a pace. Then have students read the whole words in each task and column.
- Provide repeated practice, building accuracy first, then fluency.

B1. Bossy <u>E</u>

- Have students identify how the words are the same.
- Have students identify the underlined sound and then read the word.

B2. Rhyming Words

Have students read the words and identify what's the same about them.

C1. Word Endings

Have students read any underlined word, then the word with an ending. Tell students you drop the <u>e</u> when you add -*ing* to "bake."

E1. Tricky Words

- For each Tricky Word, have students use the sounds and word parts they know to silently sound out the word. Use the word in a sentence to help with pronunciation.

laughed	When Emma snorted, everybody . . . *laughed.*
wanted	The bike was everything Amanda ever . . . *wanted.*
through	We went to the car wash and drove our car . . . *through.*
color	Green is my favorite . . . *color.*
somebody	The opposite of nobody is . . . *somebody.*

- Have students go back and read the whole words in the column.

③ MULTISYLLABIC WORDS

For each word, have students read the syllables, then the whole word. Use the word in a sentence, as appropriate.

kitchen	The chef prepared the food in the . . . *kitchen.*
rumbling	The volcano was . . . *rumbling.*
generations	My mother and grandmother belong to different . . . *generations.*
remember	They bought a souvenir so they could . . . *remember* . . . their trip.

④ SPANISH WORDS

Read each Spanish phrase using the pronunciation guide. If possible, have a Spanish-speaking student assist. Have students read each word and the translation.

⑤ GENERALIZATION: READING NEW WORDS IN PARAGRAPHS

- Have students read the paragraph silently, then out loud. Tell students to use the sounds and word parts they know to read any difficult words.
- Repeat practice, as needed.

Ricardo's Stories

Unit 9 Exercise 5a
Use before Chapter 2

1. SOUND REVIEW Use selected Sound Cards from Units 1–8.

2. ACCURACY AND FLUENCY BUILDING For each column, have students say any underlined part, then read each word. Next, have students read the whole column.

A1 Mixed Practice	B1 Bossy E	C1 Word Endings	D1 Morphographs & Affixes	E1 Tricky Words
<u>ow</u>n	b<u>i</u>te	<u>vi</u>sited	<u>re</u>trace	laughed
sh<u>oo</u>k	m<u>a</u>de	<u>wa</u>ved	final<u>ly</u>	wanted
market	h<u>o</u>me	<u>sto</u>res	help<u>ful</u>	through
fl<u>ew</u>	bes<u>i</u>de	<u>ol</u>der	expect	color
sl<u>ow</u>	**B2** Rhyming Words		<u>un</u>do	somebody
<u>o</u>ver	k<u>ind</u>	bake	kiss<u>es</u>	
slept	m<u>ind</u>	baked	sta<u>tion</u>	
	beh<u>ind</u>	baking		

3. MULTISYLLABIC WORDS Have students read each word part, then read each whole word.

A	kitch·en	kitchen	rum·bling	rumbling
B	gen·er·a·tions	generations	re·mem·ber	remember

4. SPANISH WORDS Have students read the word using the pronunciation guide. Then have students read the sentence that tells what the word means.

A	¡Qué delicioso!	kay day-lee-see-oh-soh <u>Qué</u> <u>delicioso</u> means how delicious.
B	¡Buenos días!	bway-nohs dee-ahs <u>Buenos</u> <u>días</u> means good morning.

5. GENERALIZATION Have students read the paragraph silently, then out loud. (New words: greeted, Papa, none)

My grandfather, grandmother, and other relatives came over for dinner. We greeted them at the door and gave them lots of hugs and kisses. They had just come back from a trip to Mexico. Papa baked bread and a scrumptious chocolate cake. There was none left by the end of dinner.
We all had a great time.

14

★PERSONAL NARRATIVE

PURPOSE

The purpose of this lesson is to provide explicit instruction in how to use a story frame to complete a personal narrative. The lesson prepares students for Comprehension and Skill Work. Students do not write in their books.

COMPREHENSION PROCESSES

Remember, Create

PROCEDURES

PREP NOTES

To demonstrate how to write a personal narrative, use an overhead of page 15 in student *Exercise Book 2*, write on a transparency placed over the page, or use a paper copy.

❶ **INTRODUCTION**

Explain the purpose of the lesson. Say something like:
Judith and Ricardo's stories were about experiences they had growing up. These stories are called personal narratives. A personal narrative is someone's special story. We all have personal stories that are fun to tell.

❷ **BRAINSTORMING**

Generating Ideas

Have students brainstorm ideas. Say something like: To write a personal narrative, think of a time that you like to remember. I can think of several things that I might want to write about . . . the first time I saw a baseball game, my grandmother's 80th birthday party, the first time I saw a deer . . . Partner number 1, it's your turn to tell your partner about a special time.

After a minute, say: Partner number 2, it's your turn to tell your partner about a special time.
After a minute, say: What are some things you talked about with your partner? (My sister and I went to the park and watched a puppet show. I went to camp. My family . . .)

❸ **WRITING A PERSONAL NARRATIVE**

Identifying—What

• Using the story frame, demonstrate how to write a personal narrative. Say something like:
  Read the title of the story. (One of the Best Times Ever)
  The story has been started for you. Read the first sentence, up to the comma.
  Say "blank" when you get to the line. (When I was *blank* years old)
  If I were writing a story about the first time I went to a baseball game, I would write, "When I was six years old," because that's when I first went to a baseball game.
  Write "six" in the blank.
  Read the start of my story and the rest of the sentence. There are two more blanks.
  (When I was six years old, my *blank* and I went *blank*.) I went with my family.
  Write "family" in the next blank.
  Where did we go? (to a baseball game)
  Write "to a baseball game" in the next blank.
  Now read the rest of the paragraph. (We had a great time . . .)

• For the next paragraph, repeat, adding: First, we stood in a long line to get tickets. Next, we watched the game and cheered for our team. Finally, the game was over. Our team won. It was fun.

④ USING THE CHECK AND CORRECT BOX

Demonstrate how to use the Check and Correct box to fix up errors.

Ricardo's Stories

Unit 9 **Exercise 5b** (Focus Lesson)
Use after Exercise 5a and before Chapter 2

FOCUS
LESSON
Skills and
Strategies

★Personal Narrative
My Story

One of the Best Times Ever

When I was six years old, my family

and I went to a baseball game.

We had a great time. It was one of the best times ever.

First, we stood in a long line to get tickets.

Next, we watched the game and cheered for our
team.

Finally, the game was over. Our team won. It
was fun.

**✓ Check
and Correct**

1. Do your sentences make sense? ☑
2. Do the sentences tell the story? ☑
3. Do you have a capital at the beginning of each
   sentence and a period at the end? ☑
4. Did you use your best handwriting? ☑

STOP

Don't write
in your
Exercise
Book.

Blackline Master **15**

CHAPTER 2 INSTRUCTIONS
Students read with the teacher.

COMPREHENSION PROCESSES
Remember, Understand, Apply, Evaluate

PROCEDURES

1. Reviewing Chapter 1

   Identifying—Who, Setting; Inferring; Explaining

2. Introducing Chapter 2

   Identifying—Title, Where; Predicting

Discuss the chapter title. Ask students what they think this chapter will be about.
Say something like:
Read the title of the chapter. (A Visit to Mexico)
In the last story, we heard a story that Ricardo's mother told him.

This story is about what Ricardo did when he was a boy.
Where was Ricardo born? (He was born in the United States.)
What do you think Ricardo will tell us about? (He will tell us about going to visit Mexico.)

3. First Reading
- Ask questions and discuss the story as indicated by the gray text.
- Mix group and individual turns, independent of your voice.
  Have students work toward a group accuracy goal of 0–5 errors.
  Quietly keep track of errors made by all students in the group.
- After reading the story, practice any difficult words.
  Repeat if students have not reached the accuracy goal.

4. Second Reading: Short Passage Practice: Developing Prosody
- Demonstrate expressive, fluent reading on the first paragraph. Read at a rate slightly faster than the students' rate.
- Guide practice with your voice.
- Provide individual turns while others track with their fingers and whisper read.
  Provide descriptive and positive feedback.
- Repeat with one paragraph or one page at a time.

> **CORRECTING DECODING ERRORS**
>
> During story reading, gently correct any error, then have students reread the sentence.

5. Partner or Whisper Reading: Repeated Reading

 Before beginning independent work, have students finger track and partner or whisper read.

6. Comprehension and Skill Work

Tell students they will do Comprehension and Skill Activities 9 and 10 after they read Chapter 2. Guide practice, as needed. For teacher directions, see pages 76 and 77.

7. Homework 5: Repeated Reading

WITH THE TEACHER

Chapter 2

A Visit to Mexico

¡Hola! It's Ricardo again. This story is about my mother, my grandmother, and me. When I was twelve, Mama took me to visit Mexico. When Daniel and Isabel are a little older, we also will visit Mexico.

Papa took Mama and me to the bus station. We were sad to leave Papa behind, but he had to work.

The trip to Mexico from the United States took many hours. The quiet rumbling of the bus made me drowsy. I slept for a long time. Finally, Mama shook me and said, "Ricardo, we are here!"

Why do you think the trip to Mexico made Ricardo *drowsy?*[1] What do you think Ricardo will see in Mexico?[2]

75

COMPREHENDING AS YOU GO

❶ Apply: Inferring, Explaining; Using Vocabulary—drowsy (The trip took a long time. There was little to do. The rumbling of the bus made him drowsy . . .)

❷ Apply: Predicting (Ricardo will see his grandmother and the cow . . .)

WITH THE TEACHER

The bus came to a slow stop. I looked for cows and chickens, but there were none. There were many houses, stores, and people. It looked like the United States!

My grandmother had moved to the city to be near relatives. I would not meet the cow! We greeted her with hugs and kisses. In my best Spanish, I said, "Hi, Grandmother! How have you been? I like the color of your little house."

"¡Hola, Abuela! ¿Cómo ha estado? Me gusta el color de su casita."

What do you think Ricardo is saying in Spanish?**1**

76

COMPREHENDING
AS YOU GO

1 **Apply:** Inferring, Explaining (He is saying, "Hi, Grandmother! How have you been? I like the color of your little house.")

RICARDO'S STORIES

We sat at the kitchen table. Grandmother gave us sweet bread and hot chocolate. I took a bite and said, "¡Qué delicioso!"

Grandmother smiled.

Spanish words flew back and forth. Mama said, "Do you remember that old cow?" We all laughed and laughed.

The seven days of our trip flew by. We visited relatives. We went to the market and walked through the stands. Everywhere we went, Mama waved at somebody and said, "¡Buenos días!"

Soon it was time to go home. I wanted to see Papa, but I was also sad to leave Grandmother.

Today, I make sweet bread and hot chocolate for Daniel and Isabel. When I smell the sweet bread baking, it is as if Abuela is standing beside me. It makes me feel both happy and sad.

What did Ricardo, his mother, and grandmother laugh about?[1] Why is making sweet bread and hot chocolate bittersweet for Ricardo?[2]

77

COMPREHENDING
AS YOU GO

❶ **Remember:** Identifying—What (They laughed about the old cow . . .)
❷ **Apply:** Inferring, Explaining; **Understand:** Defining and Using Vocabulary—bittersweet
(It is bittersweet because it makes him feel both happy and sad.)

WITH THE TEACHER

78

RICARDO'S STORIES

INFERENCE

1. Why do you think Ricardo is both happy and sad when he thinks about his grandmother?

INFERENCE

2. Do you think this story is bittersweet? Why or why not?

INFERENCE

3. When Ricardo smells sweet bread baking today, what do you think he thinks of?

79

① **Apply:** Inferring, Explaining (He is happy because he remembers the fun they had, but he is sad because he misses her.)

② **Apply:** Inferring, Explaining; **Understand:** Defining and Using Vocabulary—bittersweet (It is bittersweet because it makes you feel both happy and sad.)

③ **Apply:** Inferring, Explaining (He thinks of his grandmother.)

STORY COMPREHENSION AND MAZE READING

COMPREHENSION PROCESSES

Understand, Apply

Comprehension Monitoring, Test Taking

Identifying—What

Identifying—Events

Inferring; Using Vocabulary—
bittersweet

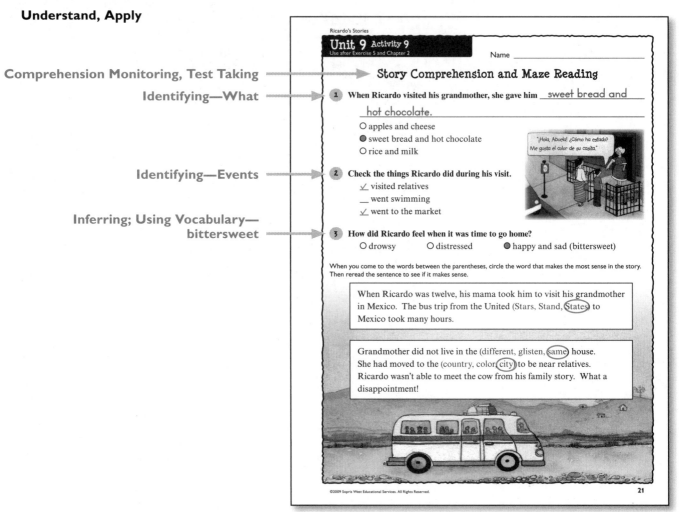

Ricardo's Stories

Unit 9 Activity 9
Use after Exercise 5 and Chapter 2

Name _____

Story Comprehension and Maze Reading

1. When Ricardo visited his grandmother, she gave him _sweet bread and hot chocolate._
   - ○ apples and cheese
   - ● sweet bread and hot chocolate
   - ○ rice and milk

   "¡Hola, Abuela! ¿Cómo ha estado?
   Me gusta el color de su casita."

2. Check the things Ricardo did during his visit.
   - ✓ visited relatives
   - ___ went swimming
   - ✓ went to the market

3. How did Ricardo feel when it was time to go home?
   - ○ drowsy   ○ distressed   ● happy and sad (bittersweet)

When you come to the words between the parentheses, circle the word that makes the most sense in the story. Then reread the sentence to see if it makes sense.

When Ricardo was twelve, his mama took him to visit his grandmother in Mexico. The bus trip from the United (Stars, Stand, **States**) to Mexico took many hours.

Grandmother did not live in the (different, glisten, **same**) house. She had moved to the (country, color, **city**) to be near relatives. Ricardo wasn't able to meet the cow from his family story. What a disappointment!

21

PROCEDURES

For each step, demonstrate and guide practice, as needed. Then have students complete the page independently.

1. **Selection Response—Basic Instructions** (Items 1–3)
   - Have students read each sentence stem or question, then fill in the bubble and blank, or check the blank with the correct answer.
   - Remind students to put a period at the end of a sentence.

2. **Maze Reading—Basic Instructions**
   - For each box, have students read the sentences and select the word in parentheses that best completes the sentence.
   - Have students circle the word, then reread the paragraph to make sure the whole paragraph makes sense.

★PERSONAL NARRATIVE • MY STORY

COMPREHENSION PROCESSES
Understand, Apply, Create

WRITING TRAITS
Ideas and Content Organization—Word Choice, Sequence Conventions—Complete Sentence, Beginning Capital, Period Presentation

Generating Ideas; Sentence Completion

Visualizing, Illustrating

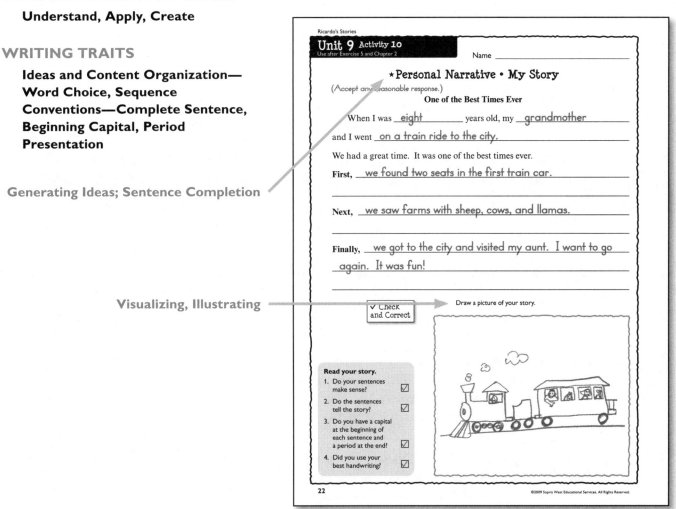

Ricardo's Stories

Unit 9 Activity 10
Use after Exercise 5 and Chapter 2

Name _____

★Personal Narrative • My Story
(Accept any reasonable response.)

One of the Best Times Ever

When I was ___eight___ years old, my ___grandmother___ and I went ___on a train ride to the city.___

We had a great time. It was one of the best times ever.

First, ___we found two seats in the first train car.___

Next, ___we saw farms with sheep, cows, and llamas.___

Finally, ___we got to the city and visited my aunt. I want to go again. It was fun!___

✓ Check and Correct

Read your story.
1. Do your sentences make sense? ☑
2. Do the sentences tell the story? ☑
3. Do you have a capital at the beginning of each sentence and a period at the end? ☑
4. Did you use your best handwriting? ☑

Draw a picture of your story.

22

PROCEDURES
For each step, demonstrate and guide practice, as needed. Then have students complete the page independently.

★1. Creative Writing: Paragraph Writing—Introductory Instructions
- Tell students they will write a personal narrative like the one they did in the Focus Lesson. (See Exercise 5b.)
- Have students brainstorm ideas for writing a personal narrative about an activity they enjoyed with their family or a friend.
- Guide students through the activity only as needed.
- Remind students to check and correct their work.

2. Illustrating—Basic Instructions
Have students draw a picture of their story.

★ = New in this unit

① SOUND REVIEW

Have students read the sounds and key word phrases. Work for accuracy, then fluency.

② SHIFTY WORD BLENDING

For each word, have students say the underlined sound. Then have them sound out the word smoothly and say it. Use the words in sentences, as appropriate.

③ SOUND PRACTICE

- For each task, have students spell and say the focus sound in the gray bar.
  Next, have students read each underlined sound two times, then the word.
  Look at the gray bar. Say o-u says /ou/ as in cloud. (o-u says /ou/ as in cloud.)
  Read each sound two times. Then say the word. (/ou/, /ou/, our; /ou/, /ou/, about . . .)
- Have students read the whole words in each column, building accuracy first, then fluency.

④ ACCURACY AND FLUENCY BUILDING

- For each task, have students say any underlined part, then read the word.
- Set a pace. Then have students read the whole words in each task and column.
- Provide repeated practice, building accuracy first, then fluency.

C1. Bossy E

For each word, have students identify the Bossy E on the end of the word. Have students identify the underlined sound and then read the word.

D1, E1. Tricky Words

- For each Tricky Word, have students use the sounds and word parts they know to silently sound out the word. Use the word in a sentence to help with pronunciation.
- If the word is unfamiliar, tell students the word. Then have students say, spell, and say it.

climb
Look at the first word. The word is *climb*. Say the word. (climb) Spell it. (c-l-i-m-b)
Let's find the tallest tree and see if we can . . . *climb* . . . it.
Read the word three times. (climb, climb, climb)

move	Tom was in my way, so I asked him to . . . *move.*
thought	Zana told everyone exactly what she . . . *thought.*
many	Juanita had eleven cats. She had . . . *many* . . . cats.
laughing	The clown was always . . . *laughing.*
eyes	As we go to sleep, we close our . . . *eyes.*
talked	I called my sister on my phone. We . . . *talked* . . . and talked.
brothers	I have many sisters and . . . *brothers.*

- Have students go back and read the whole words in each column.

⑤ MULTISYLLABIC WORDS

For each word, have students read the syllables, then the whole word.

ladder	The fireman climbed the . . . *ladder.*
stubby	Paulo's fingers were short and . . . *stubby.*
chuckle	When Barb made funny faces, her dad would always . . . *chuckle.*
fingers	On each hand, I have five . . . *fingers.*

6 MORPHOGRAPHS AND AFFIXES

- Have students read the underlined part, then the word.
- Repeat practice with whole words, mixing group and individual turns.

Fluency

Unit 9 Exercise 6
Use before Fudge

MONITORING
PROGRESS
(Reminder)

For all activities, mix group and individual turns to keep students engaged and to monitor individual performance.

1. SOUND REVIEW Have students review sounds for accuracy, then for fluency.

A	-y as in fly	all as in ball	wh as in whale	or as in horn	a_e as in cake
B	o_e	ai	-dge	ph	er

2. SHIFTY WORD BLENDING For each word, have students say the underlined part, sound out smoothly, then read the word.

look	took	shook	shake	make

3. SOUND PRACTICE For each column, have students say any underlined sound, then read each word. Next, have students read the whole column.

ou	-dge, ge	a as in ant	ow as in cow
our	Fudge	back	cow
about	page	black	shower
around	huge	grab	power
cloud	edge	ranch	brown

4. ACCURACY AND FLUENCY BUILDING For each column, have students say any underlined part, then read each word. Next, have students read the whole column.

A1 Mixed Review	B1 Mixed Review	C1 Bossy E	D1 Tricky Words	E1 Tricky Words
horse	man	rode	climb	laughing
house	mane	named	move	eyes
short	mean	times	thought	talked
shirt	main		many	brothers

5. MULTISYLLABIC WORDS Have students read each word part, then read each whole word.

A	lad•der	ladder	stub•by	stubby
B	chuck•le	chuckle	fin•gers	fingers

6. MORPHOGRAPHS AND AFFIXES Have students read each underlined word part, then the word.

powerful	noticeable	commotion	determined

FLUENCY PASSAGE INSTRUCTIONS

This Story Reading targets fluency as the primary goal of instruction and practice. Students do repeated readings of this short passage to improve accuracy, expression, and rate.

COMPREHENSION PROCESSES

Apply

PROCEDURES

1. **Warm-Up: Partner or Whisper Reading**

   Before beginning group Story Reading, have students finger track and partner or whisper read the selection.

2. **First Reading**
   - Mix group and individual turns, independent of your voice.
     Have students work toward a group accuracy goal of 0–2 errors.
     Quietly keep track of errors made by all students in the group.
   - After reading the story, practice any difficult words.
     Reread the story if students have not reached the accuracy goal.

3. **Second Reading, Short Passage Practice: Developing Prosody**
   - Demonstrate reading the first paragraph with expression and fluency. Have students finger track as you read.
   - Have students choral read the first paragraph. Encourage reading with expression and fluency.
   - Repeat with the second paragraph.

4. **Third Reading, Timed Readings: Repeated Reading**

    • Select a page. Encourage each child to work for a personal best. Have students whisper read for a one-minute Timed Reading. Tell students to go back to the top of the page and keep reading until the minute is up.
   - Have students put their finger on the last word they read and count the number of words read correctly in one minute.
   - Have students do a second Timed Reading of the same page.
   - Have students try to beat their last score.
   - Celebrate improvements.

5. **Written Assessment (Comprehension and Skill)**

   Tell students they will do a Written Assessment after they read "Fudge." For teacher directions, see pages 83 and 84.

6. **Homework 6: Repeated Reading**

WITH THE TEACHER

Fluency

Fudge

One of Papa's favorite stories was about a   8
horse named Fudge. Papa would say, "When I   16
was little, my brothers and I rode horses every   25
day. I thought the horses on our ranch were   34
very big and powerful. My favorite horse was   42
Fudge."   43

Papa would say, "That big horse, Fudge,   50
had a short black mane. He was so big that I   61
had to climb on a ladder to get on his back. I   73
would try to grab his stubby little mane, and my   83
fingers would slip.   86

"Then Fudge would move! I fell many   93
times. I think that big horse was laughing   101
at me."   103

Papa would chuckle when he talked about   110
Fudge. There was a faraway look in his eyes.   119
Sometimes I think he even looked a little sad.   128

Who do you think is the narrator in this story?**1** Who first told the story?**2**
Where do you think it took place?**3**

80

**COMPREHENDING
AS YOU GO**

PARTNER
READING—
CHECKOUT
OPPORTUNITY
While students do
Partner Reading, listen
to individuals read
the passage. Work on
accuracy and fluency, as
needed.

❶ **Apply:** Inferring—Narrator (I think Ricardo is the narrator . . .)

❷ **Apply:** Inferring—Who (Ricardo's Papa first told the story . . .)

❸ **Apply:** Inferring; Explaining—Setting (I think it took place in Mexico because that's where
Ricardo's father came from . . .)

WRITTEN ASSESSMENT

COMPREHENSION PROCESSES

Remember, Understand, Apply

WRITING TRAITS

Conventions—Complete Sentence, Capital, Period

Test Taking

Identifying—Main Character, Narrator Sentence Completion

Inferring—Main Idea

Inferring; Using Vocabulary—tradition

Defining and Using Vocabulary— commotion

Sequencing; Identifying—Action

PROCEDURES

Do not demonstrate or guide practice.

Written Assessment—Introductory Instructions

1. Introduce the Written Assessment.
   - Tell students that their work today is an opportunity for them to show what they can do independently.
   - Tell students they will whisper read the passage and then answer the questions without help.

   You're going to whisper read a passage and then answer the questions—just like you've been doing on your Comprehension and Skill Work. The only thing that is different is you need to work by yourself.
   If you read a question and aren't sure what to do, reread the question and try again.
   What should you do if you can't answer a question? (Reread the question and try again.)
   If you still can't answer the question, reread the passage and try again.
   What should you do if you still can't answer a question?
   (Reread the passage and try again.)
   If you still aren't sure, just do your best.

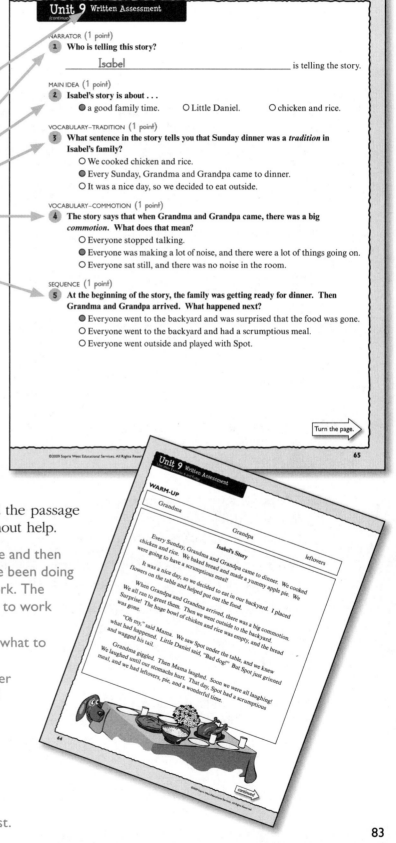

Unit 9 Written Assessment (continued)

NARRATOR (1 point)

1 Who is telling this story?

_____ Isabel _____ is telling the story.

MAIN IDEA (1 point)

2 Isabel's story is about . . .
- ● a good family time.
- ○ Little Daniel.
- ○ chicken and rice.

VOCABULARY–TRADITION (1 point)

3 What sentence in the story tells you that Sunday dinner was a *tradition* in Isabel's family?
- ○ We cooked chicken and rice.
- ● Every Sunday, Grandma and Grandpa came to dinner.
- ○ It was a nice day, so we decided to eat outside.

VOCABULARY–COMMOTION (1 point)

4 The story says that when Grandma and Grandpa came, there was a big *commotion.* What does that mean?
- ○ Everyone stopped talking.
- ● Everyone was making a lot of noise, and there were a lot of things going on.
- ○ Everyone sat still, and there was no noise in the room.

SEQUENCE (1 point)

5 At the beginning of the story, the family was getting ready for dinner. Then Grandma and Grandpa arrived. What happened next?
- ● Everyone went to the backyard and was surprised that the food was gone.
- ○ Everyone went to the backyard and had a scrumptious meal.
- ○ Everyone went outside and played with Spot.

Turn the page.

65

Unit 9 Written Assessment

WARM-UP

Grandma

Grandpa

leftovers

Isabel's Story

Every Sunday, Grandma and Grandpa came to dinner. We cooked chicken and rice. We baked bread and made a yummy apple pie. We were going to have a scrumptious meal!

It was a nice day, so we decided to eat in our backyard. I placed flowers on the table and helped put out the food.

When Grandpa and Grandma arrived, there was a big commotion. We all ran to greet them. Then we went outside to the backyard. Surprise! The huge bowl of chicken and rice was empty, and the bread was gone.

"Oh my," said Mama. We saw Spot under the table, and we knew what had happened. Little Daniel said, "Bad dog!" But Spot just grinned and wagged his tail.

Grandma giggled. Then Mama laughed. Soon we were all laughing! We laughed until our stomachs hurt. That day, Spot had a scrumptious meal, and we had leftovers, pie, and a wonderful time.

64

continued

83

WRITTEN ASSESSMENT (*continued*)

Inferring

Explaining—End, Outcome/Conclusion, Sentence Writing

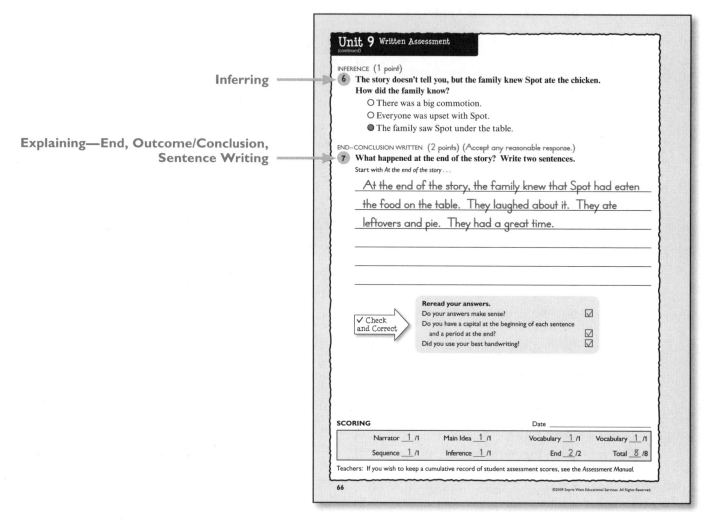

Unit 9 Written Assessment
(continued)

INFERENCE (1 point)

6 **The story doesn't tell you, but the family knew Spot ate the chicken.**
   How did the family know?
   ○ There was a big commotion.
   ○ Everyone was upset with Spot.
   ● The family saw Spot under the table.

END–CONCLUSION WRITTEN (2 points) (Accept any reasonable response.)

7 **What happened at the end of the story? Write two sentences.**
   Start with *At the end of the story . . .*

   At the end of the story, the family knew that Spot had eaten the food on the table. They laughed about it. They ate leftovers and pie. They had a great time.

✓ Check and Correct

Reread your answers.
Do your answers make sense? ☑
Do you have a capital at the beginning of each sentence
   and a period at the end? ☑
Did you use your best handwriting? ☑

SCORING   Date _____

| Narrator 1 /1 | Main Idea 1 /1 | Vocabulary 1 /1 | Vocabulary 1 /1 |
| Sequence 1 /1 | Inference 1 /1 | End 2 /2 | Total 8 /8 |

Teachers: If you wish to keep a cumulative record of student assessment scores, see the *Assessment Manual.*

66   ©2009 Sopris West Educational Services. All Rights Reserved.

2. Check for student understanding.
   Say something like:
   Look at your assessment. What are you going to do first? (write my name)

   What are going to do next? (whisper read the passage)
   What will you do after you read the passage? (answer the questions)

   That's great. Now what will you do if you get to a hard question?
   (reread the question and try again)
   That's right. What should you do if it's still hard? (reread the passage and try again)
   Very good. And if you still aren't sure, what will you do? (do my best and keep going)

3. Remind students to check and correct.
   When you finish your assessment, what should you do? (check and correct)
   That's right. Go to the top of the page. Reread the questions and make sure your answers make sense. Fix anything that doesn't sound right. Make sure you have an answer for every question.

4. Remind students what to do when they finish their work.

End of the Unit

In this section, you will find:

Making Decisions

As you near the end of the unit, plan to give the Written Assessment and the Oral Reading Fluency Assessment to each child in your group. Use this section as a general guide for making instructional decisions and doing diagnostic planning.

Written Assessment

The Unit 9 Written Assessment is located on page 63 of the activity book and on the CD.

Oral Reading Fluency Assessment

The Unit 9 Oral Reading Fluency Assessment is located on page 89 of this teacher's guide and in the *Assessment Manual*.

Certificate of Achievement

Celebrate your children's accomplishments. When your students master the unit skills, send home the Certificate of Achievement. Have students set goals for the next unit.

Making Decisions

GENERAL ASSESSMENT GUIDELINES

1. After students read Story Reading 6, "Fudge," give the group the Unit 9 Written Assessment in place of Comprehension and Skill Work. Follow the instructions on pages 83 and 84 of this guide.

2. While the group is completing the Written Assessment or any time during the day, administer the Oral Reading Fluency Assessment. Assess each student individually.

   Optional: Graph the results of the assessment. (See Unit 7 Teacher's Guide, pages 92 and 95.)
   • If the student's words correct per minute go up, congratulate the student.
   • If the student's words correct per minute go down, discuss the student's overall improvement and help him or her identify ways to improve for the next assessment.

3. Score oral fluency responses on the Student Assessment Record. Adhere to the scoring criteria in the *Assessment Manual*. Use a stopwatch to time how long it takes each student to read the Oral Reading Fluency Passage, and record errors.

USING THE WRITTEN ASSESSMENT RESULTS

Results of the Written Assessment *should not* be used to determine whether a student or group of students continues forward in the program. As long as students pass the Oral Reading Fluency Assessment, they should continue forward with the next unit.

The Written Assessment should be used to informally monitor how well students read independently and answer questions in writing. If any student has difficulty with the Written Assessment, re-administer the assessment orally.

If the student has difficulty answering the questions orally:
• Record the types of errors (e.g., main idea, sequencing, open-ended response).
• Provide explicit instruction for these types of questions during reading group, before independent work, and in tutorials, as needed.
   1) Demonstrate (or model) appropriate responses, guide practice, and provide opportunities for independent practice.
   2) For inferential questions, think aloud with students—explain how you arrive at an answer.
   3) For literal questions, teach students to reread a passage, locate information, reread the question, and respond.

At this level, if the student is able to answer the questions orally but not on paper, it may not be due to comprehension problems. The student's difficulties may be related to a lack of motivation; an inability to work independently; or a struggle with handwriting, spelling, language, or vocabulary.

USING THE ORAL READING FLUENCY RESULTS

At the end of each unit, you will need to make decisions regarding student progress. Should students go forward in the program? Does the group need more practice before proceeding? Do individuals require more assistance and practice to continue working in their group? These decisions all require use of the oral reading fluency data and professional judgment. As you analyze assessment results, watch for trends and anomalies.

See the *Assessment Manual* for detailed information and instructional recommendations. General guidelines and recommendations follow:

Strong Pass ≥ 109 WCPM 0–2 errors	• Continue with the current pace of instruction. • Have students set goals. (Until students are reading approximately 180 words correct per minute, oral reading fluency continues to be an instructional goal.)
Pass 87–108 WCPM 0–2 errors	• Continue with the current pace of instruction. Consider increasing fluency practice.
No Pass ≤ 86 WCPM	• If a child scores a No Pass but has previously passed all assessments, you may wish to advance the student to the next unit, then carefully monitor the student. • If a child scores a No Pass but has previously passed all assessments, you may wish to advance the student to the next unit and also provide additional practice opportunities. (See below.) • If a child scores two consecutive No Passes or periodic No Passes, additional practice must be provided. (See below.) • If a child scores three consecutive No Passes, the student should be placed in a lower-performing group.

RED FLAG
A No Pass is a red flag. A mild early intervention can prevent an intense and time-consuming intervention in the future.

Added Practice Options for Groups

Warm-Ups:
- Begin each lesson with Partner Reading of the previous day's homework.
- Begin each lesson with a five-minute Fluency Booster. Place copies of the Units 1–8 *Read Well* Homework in three-ring notebooks. Each day, have students begin finger tracking and whisper reading at Unit 1, Homework 1. At the end of five minutes, have students mark where they are in their notebooks. The next day, the goal is to read farther.
- Begin each Story Reading with a review of the previous day's story.
- After reading the story, include Short Passage Practice on a daily basis.

Jell-Well Reviews: A Jell-Well Review is the *Read Well* term for a review of earlier units. A Jell-Well Review is a period of time taken to celebrate what children have learned and an opportunity to firm up their foundation of learning. To complete a Jell-Well Review, take the group back to the last unit for which all students scored Strong Passes. Then quickly cycle back up. See the *Assessment Manual* for how to build a Jell-Well Review.

Added Practice Options for Individual Students

Tutorials: Set up five-minute tutorials on a daily basis with an assistant, trained volunteer, or cross-age tutor. Have the tutor provide Short Passage Practice and Timed Reading lessons.

Double Dose: Find ways to provide a double dose of *Read Well* instruction.
- Have the student work in his or her group *and* a lower-performing group.
- Have an instructional assistant, older student, or parent volunteer preview or review lessons.
- Preview new lessons or review previous lessons.

END-OF-THE-UNIT CELEBRATION

When students pass the Oral Reading Fluency Assessment, celebrate with the Certificate of Achievement on page 90.

Note: Using the Flesch-Kincaid Grade Level readability formula, the Unit 9 Assessment has a 2.4 readability level. Readability formulas provide only a rough estimate of difficulty. Just adding one or two multisyllabic words to the passage can increase the readability by one or two months.

TRICKY WORD and FOCUS SKILL WARM-UP

buy	ordinary	vegetables	knife	watch	bought

ORAL READING FLUENCY PASSAGE

A Cat Named Woody

⭐Tess lived in a small village in Mexico. Every Saturday, 10
there was an outdoor market in the center of town. Local farmers 22
would bring fruits and vegetables to sell. There were tables piled 33
high with sweet cakes for sale. You could buy flowers too. Tess 45
and her mom went to the market every week. 54

Phillip sold things at the market. He could turn ordinary 64
wood into cats, dogs, cars, or trucks. Tess liked to watch him 76
carve the wood with his sharp knife. Then he painted them in 88
bright colors. 90

Tess asked her mom for permission to buy a wood cat. 101
She bought one with a long tail and huge paws. It had big green 115
eyes. Phillip had painted the cat bright blue and yellow. 125

"What will you call the cat?" asked Phillip. 133

"His name is Woody!" said Tess. 139

ORAL READING FLUENCY	Start timing at the ⭐. Mark errors. Make a single slash in the text (/) at 60 seconds. If the student completes the passage in less than 60 seconds, have the student go back to the ⭐ and continue reading. Make a double slash (//) in the text at 60 seconds.
WCPM	Determine words correct per minute by subtracting errors from words read in 60 seconds.
STRONG PASS	The student scores no more than 2 errors on the first pass through the passage and reads 109 or more words correct per minute. Proceed to Unit 10.
PASS	The student scores no more than 2 errors on the first pass through the passage and reads 87 to 108 words correct per minute. Proceed to Unit 10.
NO PASS	The student scores 3 or more errors on the first pass through the passage and/or reads 86 or fewer words correct per minute. Consider regrouping or a Jell-Well Review.

Certificate of Achievement

This certifies that

_____

has successfully completed

Read Well 2 Unit 9 • Family Tales

on this _____ day of _____, _____.

Teacher Signature _____

Certificate of Achievement

This certifies that

_____

has successfully completed

Read Well 2 Unit 9 • Family Tales

on this _____ day of _____, _____.

Teacher Signature _____

Blackline Master